GUIDEPOSTS FOR THE SPIRIT:

Christmas Stories of Faith

Guideposts.
FOR THE
Spirit

CHRISTMAS
STORIES OF FAITH

EDITED BY JULIE K. HOGAN

Ideals Publications • Nashville, Tennessee

ISBN 0-8249-4600-6

Published by Ideals Publications, a division of Guideposts
535 Metroplex Drive, Suite 250, Nashville, Tennessee 37211

Library of Congress CIP data on file

Printed and bound in Italy

Color separations by Precision Color Graphics, Franklin, Wisconsin

10 9 8 7 6 5

Publisher, Patricia A. Pingry
Art Director, Eve DeGrie
Research Assistant, Mary P. Dunn
Copy Editor, Amy Johnson
Editorial Assistant, Patsy Jay
Designed by DeGrie, Kennedy & Associates
Paintings by Linda Nelson Stocks

ACKNOWLEDGMENTS

BUCK, PEARL S. "The Gift That Lasts a Lifetime." Reprinted by permission of Harold Ober Associates Incor-
porated. Copyright © 1955 by Pearl S. Buck. Copright renewed 1983. CALDWELL, TAYLOR. "My Christmas
Miracle." Copyright © 1961 by Taylor Caldwell. Reprinted by permission of William Morris Agency, Inc. on
behalf of the author. GRAHAM, BILLY. Adapted from "Three Symbols of Christmas." *Decision,* December
1960. Copyright © 1958 Billy Graham Evangelistic Association, used by permission. All rights reserved.
LEDERER, BILL. "Gift from a Sailor." Reprinted with permission of *The Saturday Evening Post.* Copyright ©
1963. Copyright renewed by BFL & MS, Inc. MARSHALL, PETER. "May We Keep It In Our Hearts" from *Let's
Keep Christmas.* Copyright © 1953 by Catherine Marshall. NIXON, MARGUERITE. "Unexpected Christmas"
from *Weekly Unity.* Copyright © 1965 by Weekly Unity. OURSLER, FULTON. "A String of Blue Beads." Reprinted by permission of the author's estate. Our sincere thanks to the following authors whom we were
unable to locate: Raymond Macdonald Alden for "The Night the Chimes Rang"; Cecil B. DeMille for "The
Spirit of Bethlehem"; Wanda L. Jones for "The Magic Christmas Bell"; David Niven for "In Another Stable";
Judye Reilly for "Dad's Christmas Pecans"; Dale Evans Rogers for "Christmas Is Always."

All possible care has been taken to fully acknowledge the ownership and use of every selection in
this book. If any mistakes or omissions have been inadvertently, they will be corrected in subsequent
editions, provided notification is sent to the publisher.

CONTENTS

Giving & Sharing

*Your giving is sacred and therefore should be kept a secret.
It is wise to give quietly with no strings attached.*
—CATHARINE PONDER

MARTY'S SECRET
DIANE RAYNER

I grew up believing that Christmas was a time when strange and wonderful things happened, when wise and royal visitors came riding, when at midnight the barnyard animals talked to one another, and in the light of a fabulous star God came down to us as a child. Christmas to me has always been a time of enchantment, and never more so than the year my son Marty was eight.

That was the year my children and I moved into a cozy trailerhome in a forested area just outside of Redmond, Washington. As the holiday approached, our spirits were light, not to be dampened even by the winter rains that swept down Puget Sound to douse our home and make our floors muddy.

Throughout that December, Marty had been the most spirited and busiest of us all. He was my youngest, a cheerful boy, blond and playful, with a quaint habit of looking up at you and cocking his head like a puppy when you spoke to him. The reason for this was that Marty was deaf in his left ear, but it was a condition he never complained about.

For weeks I had been watching Marty. I knew something was going on that he was not telling me about. I knew how eagerly he made his bed, took out the trash, and carefully set the table and helped Rick and Pam prepare dinner before I got home from work. I saw how he silently collected his allowance and tucked it away, not spending a cent of it. I had no idea what all this quiet activity was about, but I suspected it had something to do with Kenny.

Kenny was Marty's friend, and ever since they had found each other in the springtime, they were seldom apart. If you called to one, you got them both. Their world was in the meadow—a horse pasture broken by a small winding stream—where they caught frogs and snakes, searched for arrowheads or hidden treasure, or spent afternoons feeding peanuts to squirrels.

Times were hard for our family, and we had to do some scrimping to get by. Thanks to my job as a meat wrapper and a lot of ingenuity, we managed to have elegance on a shoestring. But not Kenny's family. They were desperately poor, and his mother was struggling to feed and clothe her two children. They were a good, solid family; but Kenny's mom was a proud woman, and she had strict rules.

How we worked, as we did each year, to make our home festive for the holiday! Ours was a handcrafted Christmas of gifts hidden away and ornaments strung about the place.

Marty and Kenny sometimes sat still at the table long enough to help make cornucopias or weave baskets for the tree; but then one whispered to the other, and they were out the door in a flash, sliding cautiously under the electric fence into the horse pasture that separated our home from Kenny's.

One night shortly before Christmas, when my hands were deep in peppernödder dough, shaping nutlike Danish cookies heavily spiced with cinnamon, Marty came to me and said in a tone mixed with pleasure and pride, "Mom, I've bought Kenny a Christmas present. Want to see it?" So that's what he's been up to, I thought. "It's something he's wanted for a long, long time, Mom."

After carefully wiping his hands on a dish towel, he pulled a small box from his pocket. Lifting the lid, I gazed at the pocket compass that my son had been saving all those allowances to buy.

"It's a lovely gift, Martin," I said, but even as I spoke, a disturbing thought came to mind. I knew how Kenny's mother felt about their poverty. They could barely afford to exchange gifts among themselves, and giving presents to others was out of the question. I was sure she would not permit her son to receive something he could not return in kind.

Gently, carefully, I talked over the problem with Marty. He understood what I was saying.

"I know, Mom, I know...but what if it was a secret? What if they never found out who gave it?"

I didn't know how to answer him.

The day before Christmas was rainy, cold, and gray. The three kids and I all but fell over one another as we elbowed our way about our home putting finishing touches on secret Christmas gifts and preparing for family and friends who would drop by.

Night settled in. The rain continued. I looked out the window over the sink and felt an odd sadness. How mundane the rain seemed for a Christmas Eve. Would wise men come on such a night? I doubted it. It seemed to me that strange and wonderful things happened only on clear nights, nights when one could at least see a star in the heavens.

I turned from the window, and as I checked on the ham and lefse bread warming in the oven, I saw Marty slip out the door. He wore his coat over his pajamas, and he clutched a tiny, colorfully wrapped box.

Down through the soggy pasture he went, then under the electric fence and across the yard to Kenny's house. Up the steps on tiptoe, shoes squishing; open the screen door just a crack; place the gift on the doorstep, then take a deep breath, reach for the doorbell and press on it hard.

Quickly Marty turned and ran down the steps and across the yard in a wild race to get away unnoticed. Then, suddenly, he banged into the electric fence.

The shock sent him reeling. He lay stunned on the wet ground. His body tingled and he gasped for breath. Then slowly, weakly, confused and frightened, he began the grueling trip back home.

"Marty," I cried as he stumbled through the door, "what happened?" His lower lip quivered, his eyes brimmed.

"I forgot about the fence, and it knocked me down!"

I hugged his muddy body to me. He was still dazed, and there was a red mark beginning to blister on his face from his mouth to his ear. Quickly I treated the blister; and with a warm cup of cocoa soothing him, Marty's bright spirits returned. I tucked him into bed and just before he fell asleep he looked up at me and said, "Mom, Kenny didn't see me. I'm sure he didn't see me."

That Christmas Eve I went to bed unhappy and puzzled. It seemed such a cruel thing to happen to a little boy who was doing what the Lord wants us all to do, giving to others, and giving in secret at that. I did not sleep well that night. Somewhere deep inside I think I must have been feeling the disappointment that Christmas had come and it had been just an ordinary, problem-filled night, no mysterious enchantment at all.

But I was wrong. By morning the rain stopped and the sun shone. The streak on Marty's face was red, but I could tell that the burn was not serious.

We opened our presents, and soon, not unexpectedly, Kenny was knocking on the door, eager to show Marty his new compass and tell about the mystery of its arrival. It was plain that Kenny didn't suspect Marty at all, and while the two of them talked, Marty just smiled and smiled.

Then I noticed that while the two boys were comparing their Christmases, nodding and gesturing and chattering away, Marty was not cocking his head when Kenny was talking. Marty seemed to be listening with his deaf ear. Weeks later a report came from the school nurse, verifying what Marty and I already knew: "Marty now has complete hearing in both ears."

How Marty regained his hearing, and still has it, remains a mystery. Doctors suspect that the shock from the electric fence was somehow responsible. Perhaps so. Whatever the reason, I am thankful to God for the good exchange of gifts that was made that night.

So you see, strange and wonderful things still happen on the night of our Lord's birth. And one does not have to have a clear night to follow a fabulous star.

When you judge people, you have no time to love them.
—MOTHER TERESA

UNCLE MAX THE MISER

RICHARD H. SCHNEIDER

hen I was eleven, I thought Uncle Max (pronounced "Mox" in my family) was the stingiest man alive. Max Maegdefessel had married my Aunt Gustie back in antiquity and was my least favorite relative. Maybe it was because of the picture of him as a young Prussian Army officer that hung in their living room. With his short-clipped iron-gray hair, toothbrush mustache and starched bearing, he epitomized the leader of the enemy troops that my lead soldiers would vanquish daily in bedroom-floor battles.

Or maybe it was because I was forced to sit through too many productions of his Richard Wagner *Gesangverein*. In this "singing society," several men, looking much like Uncle Max, stood together on a stage and, with accompanying saliva sprays, roared songs completely unintelligible to me.

But it was his miserliness that most repelled me. When we'd visit Aunt Gustie's house on Christmas Day and sing Christmas songs around the *Tannenbaum* on which candles flickered, I knew that Uncle Max had gone to the tree lot that Christmas morning and bargained for a leftover. Usually he got it for a nickel.

Our favors would be chocolate coins encased in gold tinfoil, which, judging from the odd flavor, had been bought at last year's after-Christmas sales.

But Uncle Max did have a talent. A metalsmith, with no job during the Depression, he made things for people on order. These included contrivances involving multispirals, made of copper tubing, which I vaguely understood had something to do with Prohibition. Once, he carefully shaped a silver star for his wife's Eastern Star group.

My two brothers and I would slip down into his basement, which reeked of sodden cigars, and watch him at work. Wearing a leather apron, his little round spectacles reflecting the bench light, and wielding a variety of odd-shaped hammers and anvils, he appeared oblivious to everything but his work.

On the Christmas marking my parents' fifteenth wedding anniversary year, Uncle Max and Aunt Gustie came to our house. On Christmas Eve, after a large dinner and church services, we boys dutifully recited our memorized pieces or sang songs, then rushed to our gifts. Afterward, Uncle Max said he had something for my parents.

The presentation was done with great fanfare, including a song he had to sing. I made sure I wasn't sitting in front of him. He then presented the gift to my mother. She opened the box, drew out a felt bag, undid its drawstring, and lifted out a silver teapot, at which I could not help but gasp with the rest of my family.

As my mother and father admired it, the polished teapot glinted in the tree lights. When my mother and aunt went into the kitchen to wash dishes, my father and uncle settled in easy chairs to talk. I left my windup American Flyer train and stepped over to the mantle where the teapot rested in honor. It was hexagonal, its body, spout, and handle each fashioned of six pieces of nickel silver. I knew enough to realize that Uncle Max must have made a special wooden form for each of its multishaped parts. He'd have had to work the nickel-silver sections into perfect shapes, and then carefully, meticulously solder each segment together so that the teapot appeared to be molded from one piece of silver.

I glanced over at Uncle Max, now snoring softly in his chair, and thought of the many weeks he must have spent working on his gift. It had taken precious time from their little income of filling orders for evaporators, trumpets, and decorations.

I think I grew up a little that night. Somehow Uncle Max and Aunt Gustie had been able to host others, give gifts, and donate their time, despite the fact that he'd been jobless for years. And he had done it in the only way he knew how: by saving pennies, hunting sales and, yes, bargaining at tree lots.

I felt ashamed of myself as I looked back at Uncle Max, the firelight flickering off the watch chain on his ample stomach as it rose and fell with peaceful snores.

He has been gone many years. But in my memory his teapot still sits on my mother's mantle, reminding me of important things, of simple joys, of homemade gifts in which the giver gives of himself, but most of all, of what the One whose birth we celebrate taught us: "Stop judging by mere appearances."

Some of the best lessons we ever learn, we learn from our mistakes and failures. The error of the past is the wisdom and success of the future.

—TRYON EDWARDS

IN FULL SUPPLY

JACQUELINE HEWITT ALLEN

Years and years ago, my grandmother told me a story out of her past that I always think of at gift-giving time, especially at Christmas. I remember sitting in her lap as dark-eyed little Sue Belle Johnson, my grandmother, explained how, shortly after the turn of the century, at remote and often lonely stations across the United States and overseas, missionaries and their families lived lives of hardship, privation, and isolation in their efforts to carry the gospel to people most of us would never know or see.

Probably at no time of the year were their feelings of isolation and loneliness more keenly felt than at Christmas. To remember them at this season, the custom in those days was for churches to send what were called "missionary barrels" to missionaries in remote locations.

The missionary and his wife would sit down with the children and make a list of things they wanted for Christmas. The list would include articles of clothing, toys, perhaps books or household utensils—whatever they especially needed but could not afford or could not find to buy. The list also included the ages of the children and their clothing sizes.

When completed, the list was sent to the missionary organization that helped sponsor them. The organization in turn sent it to a church, whose members would then take it upon themselves to acquire the items on the list.

My grandmother's church in Hattiesburg, Mississippi, was one of the churches that received such a Christmas list. That particular year, the list came from a missionary family in what was then called Indian Territory. Many of the women of Grandmother's church saw it as a holy task to choose an item and either buy it, make it, or donate money for its purchase.

On an appointed day, all the requested items would be brought to the church, and the women would check the items against the list and wrap them and pack them into a big wooden-staved, double-ended barrel. The barrel would then be shipped in time for the family to receive it by Christmas.

Not everybody in Grandmother's church cooperated. While the women were packing the missionary barrel, one of the more well-to-do women of the church walked into the room carrying a coat. "I've got this coat of my husband's that I want to give to you," she announced offhandedly. "I'm going to buy him a new one."

Grandmother was appalled. She didn't say anything, but she was thinking plenty. These other people have worked hard to get these articles, some have sacrificed to get them, and here this woman is in effect bragging, "I'm so rich I can go out and buy another coat."

The more she thought about the woman's haughtiness, the more irritated Grandmother became. She's just ridding herself of an unwanted castoff, Grandmother said to herself. What kind of Christmas attitude is that? Grandmother was furious—about the coat and with the woman.

A coat was not on the missionary family's list, and the women packing the barrel had no intention of putting the coat in it. But after all the requested items had been carefully placed in the barrel, there was still room left.

"Well," one of the women said, "let's put that coat in. It might help keep the other articles tight, keep them from bouncing around and maybe breaking."

So, they folded the coat, packed it in, and closed the barrel. Then they shipped it to the family out in the Indian Territory.

Weeks passed. Christmas came and went. Then a letter arrived at the church. It was the family's thank-you, written by the missionary's wife. "Dear Friends," it began, "we want to thank you for the barrel."

She then recounted how her husband and their three children had driven to the railhead to pick up the barrel, had brought it home, and had placed it upright in the middle of the living room floor in their little cabin, waiting for Christmas. The children were so excited they danced around it in gleeful anticipation.

Then on the day before Christmas, a fierce winter storm blew in. It quickly developed into a blizzard, with snow so thick and winds so furious that the entire outdoors seemed a blowing, blinding mass of white. Shortly before suppertime, as the blizzard raged, there was a banging on the front door, and when the missionary opened the door to see what the banging was, there stood an old man, grizzled, ill-clad for the freezing temperature, shivering, and covered with snow.

"I'm lost," the man said. "Could I come in for a while?"

The missionary opened the door wider and said, "Of course. Come on in."

After supper, it was all but impossible to contain the children. They were so excited and eager to open the barrel. But their mother managed to get them bedded down, explaining that they would have to wait a little longer, since it would be terribly impolite to open the barrel, pull out the presents, and distribute them with the old man there. "There's nothing for him," the mother said. "It's just the things we put on our list. We'll have to wait till the man leaves."

The next morning, Christmas morning, the family arose and found that the storm had not abated; the winds were as wild as the night before. The mother fixed a special breakfast for everyone, and when breakfast was over, they watched and waited for the storm to end so that the old man could be on his way and they could break open the barrel.

Afternoon came and the storm was still raging, but the children just couldn't wait any longer. So the missionary and his wife explained to the old man that the barrel had been packed many weeks earlier and contained Christmas presents for the family only. They apologized profusely, and when the old man nodded and said he understood, the missionary turned to the barrel and began to break open the uppermost end of it.

The family then began pulling out one by one the items they had asked for on their Christmas list. Each item was clearly marked so that they all knew whose present it was. Everyone was excited. The clothes, the toys; everything was exactly what the family had requested. Everyone was happy and pleased, while the old man sat and watched.

Finally they reached the bottom of the barrel. There on the bottom, at the end of the barrel that had been uppermost when the women packed it, was an item the family didn't recognize. It was nothing they had asked for. When the missionary reached deep into the barrel to pull out the object, he could see it was a man's coat. He held it up. It looked to be about the size of the old man. "Try it on." The man took it and slipped it on. It fit perfectly. "It must be for you," the missionary told him, smiling.

"How did you ever know," the missionary wife's letter concluded, "that we would need a man's coat for Christmas? Thank you all so very much."

By the time she finished reading the letter, my grandmother said, she was nearly overcome with awe. The cast-off coat that had needed a new owner had found one. An old man who had needed a warm coat had been given one. A family who had taken in a lost stranger and needed a special present for him had been provided with one. It was all too marvelous. God had wrought a miracle with a gift she had thought unworthy.

When she finished her story, Grandmother took my hands in hers and said, "I learned that day that I had been wrong—and that I should never despise a gift that God can use."

As Christmas approaches again, I'm remembering once more my grandmother's words. As I choose presents to give this Christmas, I am hoping that they will be gifts that will make the recipients happy and me proud to give. But most of all, I am praying that, whatever they are, whomever they're for, they will be exactly the gifts that God can use.

Every man's life is a plan of God.
—HORACE BUSHNELL

THE GREATEST GIFT OF ALL

DAN KRAINERT

I hung up the phone and turned to my parents. "Dr. Wallwork says I can go home for Christmas." We smiled at one another as if this were good news, but all three of us knew it really wasn't.

It was December 22, 1980, and for months we'd been living on what was called Life Row. These were the apartments a block from the Stanford Medical Center in Palo Alto, where patients such as I waited for organs to become available for transplant. At the age of eighteen, I was waiting for a new heart.

Mom was already on the phone to my grandmother in our house in Napa, California. "We're coming home!" she said. "Let's do Christmas right!"

The three of us packed our few belongings and climbed into our Dodge Magnum. Part of me wished it weren't the holiday. I wanted to enjoy being at home, but we all knew that without a new heart my death was imminent. What was the point in celebrating Christmas?

And yet we were going *home*. I decided to be cheerful for my family—the same decision I was certain they were making for me.

The view out the car window was welcome. Months of hospitalization are rough on anyone; but for a teenager like me, the relentless white walls and antiseptic smells had been suffocating. Now the colors, sounds, even the exhaust fumes of Highway 101, were invigorating. It had been a rough couple of years. I'd been born with a degenerative heart condition, but inexplicably it had gone into remission when I was a baby. I'd been able to live a normal life. My high school days had been filled with friends, dramatics, and baseball. Life was good.

Then in my junior year I started having massive heart failure; the remission was over. Even now, sitting in the back seat of the car, I could feel my worn-out heart beating wildly against my chest. It couldn't hold out much longer.

As the trip home stretched on, I tried to concentrate on all the good things I'd been given. First, our doctor had managed to get me into the transplant program at Stanford. Then, when it looked as if there was no way on earth to get the money for the transplant operation, the whole town of Napa had pitched in to help. There'd been bake sales and other money-raising projects. Friends, acquaintances, and even total strangers had donated blood. I wanted to be grateful for these things, but it would all be so futile if I didn't get the new heart.

Dad turned the car down the familiar roads of Napa, and soon we pulled into the driveway of our white ranch house. The front door opened and my grandmother came hurrying out.

"Go back! Go back!" she screamed.

"What?"

"They've got a heart!" she cried. "They've been trying to find you! The Highway Patrol has been after you, and it's even been on the radio!"

"They've got a heart?" Dad said, as though he couldn't believe it.

"Yes, but they can only keep it until four-thirty! And it's three-twenty-five!"

We looked at one another in shock. The drive back to Palo Alto would take an hour-and-a-half. But Grandma had thought ahead. "We've chartered a private plane," she said.

As she spoke, a patrol car pulled up. "Get in!" the officer bellowed. "We're heading for the Napa airport!"

Our race against time began. The Highway Patrol got us to the airport, and the pilot of a Cessna Skyhawk got us down to Palo Alto. An ambulance waited on the runway to rush us the final miles.

We pulled into the medical center at 4:26, with four minutes to spare!

In the prep room they began giving me the drug my body would need to keep from rejecting the new heart. Then I heard my name from a radio on the counter. The news announcer was asking his listeners to have a moment of prayer for me; my surgery was about to start. And in that moment I too prayed.

Mom and Dad were waiting with me. "I'd give anything to take your place, son," Dad said.

Mom put her ear to my pounding chest. "I can hear it," she said.

"Tomorrow it will make a different sound," I answered, and then I handed her the card that I'd been holding, the one that bore the quote from Ezekiel 36:26: "I will give you a new heart and put a new spirit in you" *(New International Version)*.

The next two days ran together as a groggy blur. The second day, I knew I was in one of the sterile intensive-care rooms for transplant recovery patients. My nurse, Seana, told me that the operation itself had been a success.

By the next day I could be propped up in bed. There was a lot of pain in my chest from the incision, but one thing was very different. For the first time in two years, I could not *feel* my heart!

My family gathered outside the glass windows of the room. They had to scrub down and wear funny-looking sterile gowns, gloves, and masks, and only two could enter at a time. But in they came!

"Dan," Mom said. "Merry Christmas!"

Christmas. It was Christmas Day. And only days before, I'd thought about the pointlessness of celebrating Christmas. Now I had all the reason in the world!

With trembling hands, Mom gave me my Bible. Together we turned to the second chapter of Luke, and everyone stood silent and let me read aloud the story of Jesus' birth.

Afterward, Seana brought a tall stack of mail that had come to me at the hospital. All those cards—many from strangers who said they were praying for me. I was truly touched. We opened them and read each one aloud.

Until I came to one with a midwestern postmark. I stopped, too choked up to speak. "Dan, what is it?" Dad asked. In a hoarse voice, I read:

> Dear Dan,
> Even though we do not know you, my husband and I feel so close to your family. Our only son, Lloyd, was your donor. Knowing that you have his heart has made our loss so much easier to bear.
> With all of our love,
> Paul and Barbara Chambers

I couldn't fight the tears any longer. And suddenly I knew more clearly than ever the real reason why I should be celebrating Christmas. In dying, the Chambers' only son had given me life. In dying, God's only Son had given us life, eternal life. Now I felt like shouting out loud my thanks that Jesus Christ was born!

"Thank You, Lord!" I said. "And bless you," I said, as I thought of the young man who had signed the donor card that gave me my greatest Christmas present of all. "Bless you, Lloyd Chambers."

The human way of growing is unique; it has no rules, and can occur in many ways.

—MARSHA SINETAR

THE FOURTH WISE MAN

LINN ANN HUNTINGTON

Looking back, I can't recall exactly who thought up the idea for the practical joke on Richie. Maybe it was Jimmy Ray or Ben. Maybe I did. It was one week after our team, the Blue Raiders, had lost the 8th grade district football title. And there was no doubt in any of our minds as to whose fault that was—Richie's.

I don't know when I first realized Richie wasn't quite like everyone else. He was a year older than the rest of us, having been held back a grade. He was a big kid who walked awkwardly and spoke haltingly.

We were behind by three points when Richie came into that game. He broke through their defensive line with no trouble at all. Jimmy Ray lofted a perfect pass and Richie stood there in the middle of the field and pulled it in. The crowd went wild, screaming "Go, Go." And maybe that's why it happened. In all the noise, Richie became confused and ran the wrong way. It was a forty-six-yard touchdown pass and Richie had scored six points for the other team.

So that's how we came to think up the joke on Richie. Every year on the day before Christmas vacation our homeroom had a Christmas party in the afternoon and the traditional pageant for our families that night. We all drew names from a box and bought an inexpensive gift for that person to exchange at the party. I drew Richie's name, and Jimmy Ray and Ben and I knew just what we'd get him. It was more expensive than the usual things, but we pooled our money. The joke on big, slow Richie would be worth it.

As we nibbled the cookies and sipped the punch the PTA provided, we could hardly wait for the gift opening. Finally our teacher, Mrs. Marlowe, announced that it was time for Santa's arrival. The principal, dressed in a Santa suit, came running in with a lot of "Ho, ho, ho's" and started picking up the packages under the tree and calling out the names. There were the usual scarves, records, and other stuff that each kid knew the other had wanted. We knew Richie wanted the gift we had for him, but he was in for a real surprise.

Finally Richie's name was called. I held my breath as he fumbled with the ribbons and paper. Then he pulled out a football. Ben had painted it a garish purple, intended to resemble our school color. The inscription in bold red letters said mockingly, "OUR HERO."

The cafeteria grew quiet. Mrs. Marlowe turned around, her face angry. Her eyes searched the room and rested on the three of us. I was trying hard to keep a straight face, but in that instant I knew she knew. And I also knew we were in for big trouble.

Richie just stood there in the middle of the room, his mouth open. He gently stroked the football, his eyes blinking behind thick glasses.

I tried to duck out of school as soon as the party was over, but Mrs. Marlowe stopped me. "I want to talk to you, Carl. Why did you do it?"

"It was just a joke," I mumbled, wishing I could fall through the floor.

"A joke!" She paused. "We'll talk about this later. I don't have time right now, but I want to see you backstage after tonight's program. Understood?" I nodded.

The Christmas pageant helped take my mind off my own problems. The Glee Club sang Christmas carols during the set changes, the candles they held flickering softly in the auditorium. From the elevated cage where I worked the lights, I had a good view of the stage. Now my spotlight focused on one single large star near the top of the backdrop. I could almost visualize how it must have been on that night long ago, how vast the sky must have looked to those shepherds tending their flocks outside Bethlehem.

Then the narrator's voice was saying, "And suddenly there was with the angel a multitude of the Heavenly host, praising God and saying, 'Glory to God in the highest, and on earth peace, good will toward men.'"

Good will toward men. The words made me wince. Mrs. Marlowe's eye caught mine and I wished I'd never seen or heard of that stupid football.

I asked one of the other guys to take over for me and I hurried toward the dressing rooms. I found Richie sitting alone in one corner, dressed as a wise man, the football in his hands.

I stood before him, hands sunk in my pockets, and took a deep breath. "Richie, I'm sorry. I was the one who gave you the football."

He looked up. "*You* gave me the football, Carl?" I nodded, my face feeling flushed. "It must have been awfully expensive, Carl. I always wanted a football. You're a good guy, Carl." Richie's face lit up and he smiled a wide smile at me.

I started to speak, but suddenly he heard his cue and hurried up to the stage. From the wings, I watched the three Wise Men make their way on stage. The first two in turn presented their gifts of gold and frankincense. Then it was Richie's turn. Carefully he stepped to the manger.

"This gift I bring to the baby Jesus," he began. Then he paused. The crowd stirred uneasily. "This gift I bring to the baby Jesus," he said again. And from the folds of his robe he withdrew the gift. But it wasn't the expected flask of myrrh. I gasped along with the audience as Richie held up his purple football.

"I've always wanted a football of my very own," he said quietly to the doll inside the manger. "My friend Carl got me this one." He looked out to the audience. "This football means a lot to me," he stammered. "But I want to give it to the Baby Jesus." Gently he laid the ball in the manger.

The auditorium was silent as the curtain closed. Then the audience exploded into applause. Richie came up to me, his fake beard slightly askew. "You don't mind that I gave the football away, do you, Carl?"

I shook my head, trying to dislodge the lump in my throat.

"Carl, those words on the football. What did that one word say? H-E-R-O. What does that mean?"

I struggled to find the right words. "A hero is someone everybody looks up to."

He looked surprised. "Does everyone look up to me, Carl?"

I put my hand to his shoulder, then helped him straighten his crooked beard. "Yes, Richie, tonight you're everyone's hero. Just listen to that crowd. They're applauding you."

He listened and his face broke into a wide grin. I pushed him on stage for his curtain call. Mrs. Marlowe came and stood beside me.

"I heard what you told Richie," she said, smiling at me. "I think he was probably the wisest of our three Wise Men tonight. But you know," she added, smiling at me, "I think maybe now there's a fourth one."

When you think everything is hopeless, a little ray of light comes from somewhere.
—GERMAN PROVERB

THE GLOW ACROSS THE FIELD

CARMEN ROBERTSON

I sat at the kitchen table Christmas Eve morning staring out the window at the wide frozen field that separated our house from our neighbor Mrs. Houston's. *If only Daddy were home.* This was the night he would set me on his lap and read to me about the angels that visited the shepherds on the first Christmas Eve. Then we'd look out across the field and pretend we saw angels in every shooting star and shadowy bird, even in the faint wisps of smoke curling up from Mrs. Houston's chimney. And we'd make believe that the cheery orange glow from her house was some shepherd's campfire.

But it was 1941 and Daddy was in the Army. We hadn't heard from him in weeks, and I was worried because of the news on the radio. Mother had taken work as a clerk to keep us fed and clothed. There was a sad weariness in her eyes that kept me from asking her to make divinity or gingerbread men. Instead I tried to make the cookies myself, but they came out sad-looking too, with droopy raisin mouths and wrinkled brows.

We didn't even have a Christmas tree; my older brother, Carson, who usually made a fuss over finding the perfect one, didn't seem to care. All that tough year I had looked forward to the magic of Christmastime. Yet now there was only gloomy emptiness. Perhaps the war raging in Europe had scared off even the imaginary angels.

"Carmen," my mother called from the couch. I went to her and she handed me a five-dollar bill. "Go to the store and buy each of us a present." She gave me a tired pat on the arm and returned to her mending.

I put on my coat and mittens and tucked the five-dollar bill into my pocket. I should have been excited that Mother was treating me as a grown-up. After all, at age eleven, I'd "known" about Santa Claus for some time. Still, I would have preferred the excitement of unwrapping a surprise gift.

I kept my mittened hand wrapped tightly around the money as I started out across the icy field toward the general store two miles away. The trees reached out their bare limbs to the stony sky. Mounds of snow remained at the bottom of old cornstalks. The wind whipped at my back, blowing my hair into my eyes. I started to think about what to get for Mother and Carson. Maybe they'd smile when they opened their gifts. Maybe we'd laugh and talk and sing carols. Maybe Christmas would feel like Christmas again.

A rabbit darted out from one of the clumps of snow into my path. Startled, I slipped and fell to the hard-packed ground. I got up and rubbed my knee, blinking back tears.

Through the trees I spied a curl of blue-gray smoke rising from Mrs. Houston's chimney. *She's probably making gingerbread cookies right now*, I thought. *Happy ones*. I remembered the time when, inspired by Daddy and our Christmas ritual, I had ventured close to her house to search for campfire ashes and sheep tracks. Mrs. Houston had come out, tall and broad-shouldered, dressed in a crisp brown-and-white-checked pinafore. I froze, afraid she'd be mad. But she had looked at me with kind eyes and invited me in for some cookies and cocoa. "I'm so glad you came," she said, giving me a big hug as if she'd known me forever.

Standing there looking at her house now, with a knee that felt as though it had been skinned, and nose and ears numb from the cold, I wanted nothing more than to be sitting in her warm kitchen, eating Christmas cookies. Somehow it seemed that being with her would make everything cheerful again. But I had grown-up responsibilities and there wasn't time to dawdle. I hurried on.

In town, people carrying wrapped packages and sacks of groceries wished each other happy holidays. I ran up the steps to the general store. It smelled of cedar and oranges. Music played from a radio on the counter. I fingered scarves and neckties, sniffed at bottles of perfume, looked longingly at a basket of Brazil nuts. Five dollars would never be enough for all I wanted to buy. I dug my hand into my pocket. It was empty. The five-dollar bill! I checked my other pocket, whisked off my mittens to see if it had slipped into one of them. Nothing. Panic welled inside me.

Frantically I unbuttoned my coat and flung it to the floor, checked the pockets of my dress, then turned my coat pockets inside out. I ran around the store, checking under tables, on shelves, inside boxes, scarcely noticing the stares of other customers. Then I knocked over the basket of Brazil nuts. When the man behind the counter came over, I grabbed his arm. "My five-dollar bill! Have you seen it?"

He shook his head, bewildered. I ran out onto the store porch and asked everyone if they'd seen my money. A couple of people shook their heads sympathetically, saying, "Sorry, kid." Others shrugged as if to say "tough luck."

I finally went back inside the store. As the radio blared "Joy to the World," I replaced the scattered nuts. I picked up my coat and put it back on, buttoning it meticulously as if that would make up for my carelessness with the money. There was news about the war, then a song about angels singing. I need an angel now, I thought. I wiped the tears from my eyes, and slowly, methodically, began to retrace my steps home, searching for the money.

The sun had started to set, muted by a cluster of clouds. Wind stung my face. I squinted at Mrs. Houston's house in the distance and rubbed my smarting knee. That's it, I realized. I must have jerked my hand out of my pocket to catch myself when I fell. I followed the rabbit's tracks as far as they were visible. I should have been more careful, I chided myself. I've ruined everything.

The sunlight was fading rapidly now, the first evening star shining faintly. I had to go home. What had I been expecting—some Christmas miracle? An angel swooping down to make Christmas happy again? No tree. No ginger-bread men. And now no gifts. Obviously God wasn't sending any angels either. I trudged home, feeling as if I had lost much more than a five-dollar bill.

I walked into the house and immediately confessed, "I lost the money," so ashamed I didn't care what my punishment would be. But Mother said nothing. Neither did Carson. I wished they would. Perhaps they'd given up on Christmas too. We barely spoke during dinner. After Mother and Carson had gone to their rooms, I stayed at the kitchen table alone in the dark. The distant glow from Mrs. Houston's house and the few weakly glittering stars did little to lighten the somber sky. I tried to imagine a shepherd's campfire, feel the awe I always felt when Daddy told the Christmas story, but I couldn't. Santa Claus, angels, peace on earth—they were all part of a fairy tale. I crept to bed.

The next morning I rolled wearily out from under my covers and went to the kitchen. Mother was heating water to wash some sheets. *Christmas is, after all, just another day,* I told myself. I looked out the window to see if the weather was all right for hanging the laundry. Bright sunshine reflected off the frost-covered field. A moving shape in the distance caught my attention and I watched it curiously. Soon I recognized Mrs. Houston. Was she coming over here? She'd never visited our house before.

"Mother, come look." She joined me at the window, then went to open the door.

"Merry Christmas," Mrs. Houston announced, setting a lumpy cloth sack on the linoleum floor. Mother started up the coffeepot and Carson took Mrs. Houston's coat. Beneath it she wore the same pinafore I remembered, the shoulder ruffles standing up stiffly like little wings.

Mrs. Houston removed three small packages from the bag and handed one to each of us. We stood there, speechless. Finally Mother cleared her throat and softly said, "We don't have anything for you."

"Your gift is just being here so I have someone to give to," Mrs. Houston replied, smiling. Suddenly our kitchen felt as warm as hers did that day I visited. "Now open your packages, all of you, and enjoy!"

For Mother there was a red can of Mavis talcum powder. Carson's gift was a comb and brush set. I carefully unwrapped the colorful paper from my box and smoothed out the ribbon, prolonging the moment. At last I took out a small brown purse with a gold-colored chain. I wouldn't lose another five-dollar bill, that was for sure.

Mother, eyes shining, looked at our guest and declared, "Mrs. Houston, you are an angel." An angel? I turned to look at Mrs. Houston as well. Yes, she must be. How else could she have known to come this particular Christmas? How else could it seem as if a fire had just been rekindled? "Won't you stay for a while?" Mother said to Mrs. Houston. "You can help me make the divinity."

Carson took the ax and went to chop down a cedar tree. I made paper chains for decoration. "Jingle Bells" played loudly on the radio, Mother and Mrs. Houston singing along as they took turns beating the egg whites. Christmas had come after all. I knew I would never again lose my faith in its promises of good will, of joyous surprises, of hope.

When Dad returned home a few months later, I told him all about our Christmas with Mrs. Houston. I climbed onto his lap and we gazed out across the field and shook our heads in wonder. We agreed that we had spent all those years imagining angels in the sky when there had been a real one right next door.

You do not have to be rich to be generous. If you have the spirit of true generosity, a pauper can give like a prince.
—CORINNE U. WILLS

THE NIGHT THE CHIMES RANG

RAYMOND MACDONALD ALDEN

Once, long ago, a magnificent church stood on a high hill in a great city. When lighted up for a special festival, it could be seen for miles around. And yet there was something even more remarkable about this church than its beauty—the strange and wonderful legend of the bells.

At one corner of the church was a tall gray tower, and at the top of the tower—so people said—was a chime of the most beautiful bells in the world. But the fact was that no one had heard the bells for many years. Not even on Christmas. For it was the custom on Christmas Eve for all the people to bring to the church their offerings to the Christ-child. And there had been a time when a very unusual offering laid on the altar brought glorious music from the chimes far up in the tower. Some said that the wind rang them, and others that the angels set them swinging. But lately no offering had been great enough to deserve the music of the chimes.

Now a few miles from the city, in a small village, lived a boy named Pedro, and his little brother. They knew very little about the Christmas chimes, but they had heard of the service in the church on Christmas Eve, and they decided to go to see the beautiful celebration.

The day before Christmas was bitterly cold, with a hard white crust on the ground. Pedro and Little Brother started out early in the afternoon, and despite the cold they reached the edge of the city by nightfall. They were about to enter one of the great gates when Pedro saw something dark on the snow near their path.

It was a poor woman who had fallen just outside the city, too sick and tired to get in where she might have found shelter. Pedro tried to rouse her, but she was barely conscious. "It's no use, Little Brother. You will have to go alone."

"Without you?" cried Little Brother.

Pedro nodded slowly. "This poor woman will freeze to death if nobody cares for her. Everyone has probably gone to the church by now, but when you come back be sure and bring someone to help her. I will stay here and try to keep her from freezing, and perhaps get her to eat the roll I have in my pocket."

"But I can't leave you!" cried Little Brother.

"Both of us need not miss the service," said Pedro. "You must see and hear everything twice, Little Brother—once for you and once for me. I am sure the Christ-child knows how I would love to worship Him. And if you get a chance, Little Brother, take this silver piece of mine and, when no one is looking, lay it down for my offering."

In this way he hurried Little Brother off to the city and blinked hard to keep back the tears of disappointment.

The great church was a brilliant place that night; it had never looked so beautiful before. When the organ played and the thousands of people sang, the walls shook with the sound.

At the close of the service came the procession with the offerings to be laid on the altar. Some brought wonderful jewels, some heavy baskets of gold. A famous writer laid down a book which he had been writing for years. And last of all walked the king of the country, hoping with all the rest to win for himself the chime of the Christmas bells.

A great murmur went through the church as the king took from his head the royal crown, all set with precious stones, and laid it on the altar. "Surely," everyone said, "we shall hear the bells now!"

But only the cold wind was heard in the tower.

The procession was over, and the choir began the closing hymn. Suddenly the organist stopped playing. The singing ceased. Not a sound could be heard from anyone in the church. As all the people strained their ears to listen, there came—softly, but distinctly—the sound of the chimes in the tower. So far away and yet so clear, the music seemed so much sweeter than anything ever heard before.

Then they all stood up together and looked at the altar to see what great gift had awakened the long-silent bells. But all they saw was the childish figure of Little Brother, who had crept softly down the aisle when no one was looking and had laid Pedro's little piece of silver on the altar.

Doing good to others is not a duty.
It is a joy, for it increases your own health and happiness.
—ZOROASTER

A GIFT FOR ANTONIO

BETTY R. GRAHAM

He walked timidly up the front steps, an incredibly small, dirty, ragged child, shoeless and with a battered gray shoebox hanging by a worn leather strap from one shoulder. He seemed so small—hardly larger than my five-year-old—as he stretched to find the doorbell. I watched as my very large Honduran maid answered the door. "*Sí?*" she boomed impatiently.

"*Zapatos?*" (shoes) he whispered.

"No!" she answered.

Something about that little brown face peering up through the iron grillwork of my front porch and the huge stern face glowering down at him jarred my maternal instinct.

"Wait, Elena," I interrupted. "I do have some shoes he can polish."

Why this boy? I thought, as I selected some shoes to offer him. What had moved me about that tiny figure, so similar to the hundreds of other beggar children I'd seen at my door in the year since our family had come to live in Honduras? Why should the impersonal attitude I'd had to strive hard to achieve in order to survive emotionally in a poverty-filled country suddenly shatter at the sight of this one waif seeking work? That's it! He wasn't begging, though heaven knows he was every bit as shabbily attired as the others. He was asking for work—not a handout.

Try as I might, I couldn't help comparing him with Brian, our healthy, well-nourished youngster. The thought of my own little one in the horrible position of having to go out on the streets to earn a living was something my middle-class American upbringing wouldn't allow me to comprehend, let alone accept. It might be easy to picture Brian in a youthful game, with his father's shoeshine box under his arm, happily offering to polish my neighbor's shoes for a few pennies. But the idea of him pleading for work to earn enough for one meal a day—and maybe going hungry if he didn't succeed—was so repulsive to me that I quickly gathered up every shoe that even hinted it had been worn.

In the months that followed, Antonio became our regular weekly visitor. He worked diligently and long on each shoe, using his finger to spread the polish from minute rouge-sized cans. I'd never seen shoe polish sold in such a small container, and I realized Antonio must buy his supplies from his meager earnings.

Brian liked him and was more successful than the rest of us in getting him to relax a little and smile, though not even Brian could distract him until his job was finished.

Elena, whose stern countenance was an attempt to conceal a warm heart, always brought him a huge plate of rice, beans, tortillas, and leftover meat. She would chat with him while he ate and thus learned that, though he was not much bigger than Brian, he was actually eleven years old, the oldest of five children, fatherless and with an invalid mother. He was the sole support of his entire family. I could hardly believe that this tiny child was only a year younger than our other son, Bruce, who looked much older and stronger.

When December came, the whole family, including Elena, discussed what gift we could give Antonio for Christmas. It shouldn't have been difficult—he had so little. But we wanted it to be something special—something he would like very much. Yet it was not an easy decision, since in all those months that he had worked for us, Antonio had never once asked for a thing from us except our business. We agreed to let Elena be our detective and try to uncover his innermost desires. Bruce and Brian were convinced that he must want toys or candy, but Elena reported that Antonio's dream was to have a new pair of long trousers.

"Shucks, that's nothing," said Bruce. "I have a whole drawer full of clothes that don't fit me any more." I tended to agree with him. Clothes had been on my list from the start, and we would give him some things Bruce had outgrown. But we wanted to give him something extra—something new.

Then Elena's native wisdom came through.

"*Señora*," she offered, "don't give him something to play with. He's a very proud little man—*hombre*. Give him something he can use."

"I've got it, Mom!" cried Bruce. "Let's give him a new shoeshine kit. His is so old and ugly."

It was decided. Now we must plan it. It must be large enough to hold the larger, more economical cans of polish, plus brushes and buffers, which Antonio didn't then possess, and it must be brightly colored and cheerful. Elena knew of a carpenter who could make such a box for us.

That week was a joy. Every one of us was enthusiastically involved. When the carpenter presented the unpainted box, we could hardly wait to paint it and shop for the necessary items to go inside it. We chose a spray can of light green paint and the largest cans of polish in every color available. It was one of the happiest times I can remember—all the family together wholehearted-ly trying to make someone else happy. Even Brian was able to do his share. After Bruce painted the box, Brian spent hours going through magazines for pictures of birds and flowers to cut out and glue on its sides. When it was all finished we stood around the table admiring it. There was no doubt in our minds that there was no finer shoebox anywhere.

"Mom, it's great!" said Bruce, frowning. "But what if somebody steals it?"

It made me proud to think that my spoiled, sometimes selfish twelve-year-old was concerned about a poor little Honduran boy's fate. Yet I knew his reasoning was sound. In a place where poverty abounds, the smaller child often falls prey to the older, bigger children. We had to devise a plan to protect Antonio.

In jet black paint we stenciled ANTONIO CRUZ across the front of the shoebox and smugly agreed we'd done our best to thwart prospective thieves.

I don't know how we were able to keep our secret from the shoeshine boy until Christmas Eve, but we did. Early on the 24th, Bruce polished all the shoes in the house so there would be no work awaiting Antonio. When I offered him Antonio's usual fee, he put it neatly on top of the wrapped present under the tree. Brian jumped up and down when the doorbell rang. "Oh, I hope he likes it," he squealed.

Elena opened the door and invited Antonio inside. He stood very still, bewildered. Never before had he set foot inside our house. He always sat on the front steps to work. Elena prodded him into the living room where a mound of presents lay underneath our giant Christmas tree. Three grinning, excited Grahams were staring at him, and he didn't understand what was happening.

"Antonio," I said, "*San Nicolas* came early and left some gifts for you." I reached down and drew out our wrapped offerings. We had wrapped each item in a separate package, remembering that half the fun is in the opening.

He stood rigid, near the door, eyes wide, without smiling. If anything, his look registered fear, not joy.

"Open them! Open them!" shouted Brian as Antonio made no move to disturb the ribbons and paper. Prodded by us all, he opened the package of clothes slowly, carefully trying not to tear the paper; and just as carefully he rewrapped it. There was no change in his expression. I pushed the other small gifts at him, helping with the opening, and again noted nothing joyful in his eyes.

"This is the best of all," shouted Bruce, grabbing the shoebox and almost throwing it at Antonio. We were so keyed up that we must have seemed like maniacs to that small, quiet boy. We hovered over him as he painstakingly removed the wrappings on our treasure. Again there was nothing but nervousness emanating from Antonio.

"Say thank you, Antonio," interrupted Elena in her normal gruff manner.

"*Gracias*," whispered the child, edging closer to the door.

Bruce looked at me, puzzled. I knew exactly what was bothering him because I felt the same disappointment. What had we done wrong?

Sensing that our little friend would continue to be miserable the longer we kept him on display, I helped him to gather his gifts together, put Bruce's money in his hand, and opened the door so he could leave. Elena came bustling from the kitchen with his dinner—a double portion of everything—

already wrapped in aluminum foil.

Antonio almost ran down the steps and into the street without a backward glance. He couldn't get away fast enough.

What can I tell the boys? I thought. *They tried so hard and gave so willingly.*

In the living room I put an arm around each silent, disappointed son. "Cheer up!" I began. "I'm sure Antonio liked your gifts. It's just that we were expecting him to get all excited, as we would have. Maybe he can't express his happiness in the same way we do. I know inside he was very pleased, but what is more important is that we all felt happy doing this for him."

Just then we caught a glimpse of Antonio through our huge circular window. He was sitting on the curb across the street. He had placed all his gifts on the sidewalk beside him. One by one he picked them up, stroking them, fondling them, savoring them. His face was bright with a joy I can't describe. The hot Honduran sun glistened as it shone on the tears running down his brown cheeks.

"Feliz Navidad—Merry Christmas, boys," I said, hugging them to me, "and to you, too, Antonio."

*They who scatter with one hand, gather with two,
not always in coin, but in kind.
Nothing multiplies so much as kindness.*

−JOHN WRAY

GIFT FROM A SAILOR

BILL LEDERER

Admiral David L. McDonald, U.S.N.
Chief of Naval Operations Washington 25, D.C.
Dear Admiral McDonald:

Eighteen people asked me to write this letter to you.

Last year at Christmas time my wife, our three boys, and I were in France, on our way from Paris to Nice in a rented car. For five wretched days everything had gone wrong. On Christmas Eve, when we checked into our hotel in Nice, there was no Christmas spirit in our hearts.

It was raining and cold when we went out to eat. We found a drab little restaurant shoddily decorated for the holiday. Only five tables were occupied. There were two German couples, two French families, and an American sailor by himself. In the corner a piano player listlessly played Christmas music.

I was too tired and miserable to care. I noticed that the other customers were eating in stony silence. The only person who seemed happy was the American sailor. While eating, he was writing a letter.

My wife ordered our meal in French. The waiter brought us the wrong thing. I scolded my wife for being stupid.

Then, at the table with the French family on our left, the father slapped one of his children for some minor infraction, and the boy began to cry.

On our right, the German wife began berating her husband.

All of us were interrupted by an unpleasant blast of cold air. Through the front door came an old flower woman. She wore a dripping, tattered overcoat and shuffled in on wet, rundown shoes. She went from one table to the other.

"Flowers, *Monsieur*? Only one *franc*." No one bought any.

Wearily she sat down at a table between the sailor and us. To the waiter she said, "A bowl of soup. I haven't sold a flower all afternoon." To the piano player she said hoarsely, "Can you imagine, Joseph, soup on Christmas Eve?"

He pointed to his empty "tipping plate."

The young sailor finished his meal and got up. Putting on his coat, he walked over to the flower woman's table.

"Happy Christmas," he said, smiling and picking out two corsages. "How much are they?"

"Two *francs, Monsieur.*"

Pressing one of the small corsages flat, he put it into the letter he had written, then handed the woman a 20-franc note.

"I don't have change, *Monsieur*," she said. "I'll get some from the waiter."

"No, Ma'am," said the sailor, leaning over and kissing the ancient cheek. "This is my Christmas present to you."

Then he came to our table, holding the other corsage in front of him. "Sir," he said to me, "may I have permission to present these flowers to your beautiful daughter?"

In one quick motion he gave my wife the corsage, wished us a Merry

Christmas, and departed. Everyone had stopped eating. Everyone had been watching the sailor.

A few seconds later, Christmas exploded throughout the restaurant like a bomb.

The old flower woman jumped up, waving the 20-franc note, and shouted to the piano player, "Joseph, my Christmas present! And you shall have half so you can have a feast too."

The piano player began to belt out *Good King Wenceslaus*.

My wife waved her corsage in time to the music. She appeared twenty years younger. She began to sing, and our three sons joined her, bellowing with enthusiasm.

"*Gut! Gut!*" shouted the Germans. They began singing in German.

The waiter embraced the flower woman. Waving their arms, they sang in French.

The Frenchman who had slapped the boy beat rhythm with his fork against a glass. The lad, now on his lap, sang in a youthful soprano.

A few hours earlier eighteen persons had been spending a miserable evening. It ended up being the happiest, the very best Christmas Eve they had ever experienced.

This, Admiral McDonald, is what I am writing you about. As the top man in the Navy, you should know about the very special gift that the U.S. Navy gave to my family, to me, and to the other people in that French restaurant. Because your young sailor had Christmas spirit in his soul, he released the love and joy that had been smothered within us by anger and disappointment. He gave us Christmas.

Thank you, Sir, and Merry Christmas!

Family & Traditions

©Linda Nelson Stocks
1994

The real voyage of discovery consists not in seeking new landscapes but in having new eyes.
–MARCEL PROUST

THE YEAR WE HAD A "SENSIBLE" CHRISTMAS

HENRY APPERS

For as long as I could remember, our family had talked about a sensible Christmas. Every year, my mother would limp home from shopping or she would sit beside the kitchen table after hours of baking, close her eyes, catch her breath, and say, "This is the last time I'm going to exhaust myself with all this holiday fuss. Next year we're going to have a *sensible* Christmas."

And always my father, if he was within earshot, would agree. "It's not worth the time and expense," he would say.

While we were kids, my sister and I lived in dread that Mom and Dad would go through with their rash vows of a reduced Christmas. But if they ever *did*, we reasoned, there were several things about Christmas that we, ourselves, would like to amend. And two of these were, namely, my mother's Uncle Lloyd and his wife, Aunt Amelia.

Many a time Lizzie and I wondered why families had to have relatives, and especially why it was our fate to inherit Uncle Lloyd and Aunt Amelia. They were a sour and formal pair who came to us every Christmas, bringing Lizzie and me handkerchiefs as gifts and expecting in return silence, respect, service, and for me to surrender my bedroom.

Lizzie and I had understood early that Great-uncle Lloyd was, indeed, a poor man, and we were sympathetic to this. But we dared to think that even poverty provided no permit for them to be stiff and cold and a nuisance in the bargain. Still, we accepted Great-uncle Lloyd and Great-aunt Amelia as our lot; and they were, for years, as much the tradition of Christmas as mistletoe.

Then came my first year in college. It must have been some perverse reaction to my being away, but Mom started it. This was to be the year of the sensible Christmas. "By not exhausting ourselves with all the folderol," she wrote me, "we'll at last have the energy and the time to *appreciate* Christmas."

Dad, as usual, went along with Mom, but added his own touch. We were not to spend more than a dollar for each of our gifts to one another. "For once," Dad said, "we'll worry about the thought behind the gift, and not about its price."

It was I who suggested that our sensible Christmas be limited to the immediate family, just the four of us. The motion was carried. Mom wrote a gracious letter to Great-uncle Lloyd explaining that what with my being away in school and for one reason and another we weren't going to do much about Christmas, so maybe they would enjoy it more if they didn't make their usual great effort to come. Dad enclosed a check, an unexpected boon.

I arrived home from college that Christmas wondering what to expect. A wreath on the front door provided a fitting nod to the season. There was a Christmas tree in the living room, and I must admit that, at first, it made my heart twinge. Artificial, the tree was small and seemed without character when compared to the luxurious, forest-smelling firs of former years. But the more I looked at it, with our brightly wrapped dollar gifts under it, the friendlier it became, and I began to think of the mess of real trees, and their fire threat, and how ridiculous, how really unnatural it was to bring a living tree inside a house anyway. Already the idea of a sensible Christmas was getting to me.

On Christmas Eve, Mom cooked a good but simple dinner, and afterward we all sat together in the living room. "This is nice," Lizzie purred, a-snuggle in the big cabbage rose chair.

"Yes," Dad agreed. "It's quiet. I'm not tired out. For once, I think I can stay awake until church."

"If this were last Christmas," I reminded Mom, "you'd still be in the kitchen with your hours of 'last-minute' jobs. More cookies. More fruit cake." I recalled the compulsive way I used to nibble at Mom's fruit cake. "But I never really liked it," I confessed with a laugh.

"I didn't know that," Mom said. She was thoughtful for a moment. Then her face brightened. "But Aunt Amelia—how she adored it!"

"Maybe she was just being nice," Lizzie said undiplomatically.

Then we fell silent. Gradually we took to reading. Dad did slip off into a short snooze before church.

Christmas morning we slept late, and once up we breakfasted before advancing to our gifts. And what a time we had with those! We laughed merrily at our own originality and cleverness. I gave Mom a cluster-pin that I had fashioned out of aluminum measuring spoons and had adorned with rhinestones. Mother wore the pin all day, or at least until we went out to Dempsey's.

At Dempsey's, the best restaurant in town, we had a wonderful, unrushed feast. There was only one awkward moment just after the consomme was served. We started to lift our spoons. Then Dad suggested that we say grace and we all started to hold hands around the table as we always do at home, and then we hesitated and drew our hands back, and then in unison we refused to be intimidated by a public eating place and held hands and said grace.

Nothing much happened the rest of the day. In the evening I wandered into the kitchen, opened the refrigerator, poked around for a minute, then closed the door and came back to the living room.

"That's a joke," I reported, with no idea at all of the effect my next remark would have. "I went out to pick at the turkey."

In tones that had no color, Mother spoke. "I knew that's what you went out there for. I've been waiting for it to happen."

No longer could she stay the sobs that now burst forth from her. "Kate!" Dad cried, rushing to her.

"Forgive me. Forgive me," Mom kept muttering.

"For what, dear? Please tell us."

"For this terrible, dreadful, sensible Christmas."

Each of us knew what she meant. Our Christmas had been as artificial as that Christmas tree; at some point the spirit of the day had just quietly crept away from us. In our efforts at common sense we had lost the reason for Christmas and had forgotten about others; this denied Him whose birthday it was all about. Each of us, we knew full well, had contributed to this selfishness, but Mom was taking the blame.

As her sobs became sniffles and our assurances began to take effect, Mom addressed us more coherently, in Mom's own special incoherent way. "I should have been in the kitchen last night instead of wasting my time," she began, covering up her sentimentality with anger. "So you don't like my fruit cake, Harry? Too bad. Aunt Amelia really adores it! And Elizabeth, even if she doesn't, you shouldn't be disrespectful to the old soul. Do you know who else loves my fruit cake? Mrs. Donegan down the street. And she didn't get her gift from me this year. Why? Because we're being *sensible*." Then Mom turned on Dad, wagging her finger at him. "We can't afford to save on Christmas, Lewis! It shuts off the heart."

That seemed to sum it up.

Yet Lizzie had another way of saying it. She put it in a letter to me at school, a letter as lovely as Lizzie herself. "Mom feels," Lizzie wrote, "that the strains and stresses are the birth pangs of Christmas. So do I. I'm certain that it is out of our efforts and tiredness and turmoil that some sudden, quiet, shining, priceless thing occurs each year, and if all we produce is only a feeling as long as a flicker, it is worth the bother."

Just as my family came to call that The Christmas That Never Was, the next one became the Prodigal Christmas. It was the most festive, and the most frazzling, time in our family's history—not because we spent any more money, but because we threw all of ourselves into the joy of Christmas. In the woods at the edge of town we cut the largest tree we'd ever had. Lizzie and I swathed the house in greens. Delicious smells came from the kitchen as Mom baked and baked and baked. . . We laughed and sang carols and joked. Even that dour pair, Great-uncle Lloyd and Great- aunt Amelia, were almost, but not quite, gay. Still, it was through them that I felt that quick surge of warmth, that glorious "feeling as long as a flicker," that made Christmas meaningful.

We had just sat down in our own dining room and had reached out our hands to one another for our circle of grace. When I took Great-aunt Amelia's hand in mine, it happened. I learned something about her, and about giving, that without this Christmas I might never have known.

The hand that I held was cold. I became aware of how gnarled her fingers were, how years of agonizing arthritis had twisted them. Only then did I think of the handkerchiefs that Lizzie and I had received this year, as in all the years before. For the first time, I saw clearly the delicate embroidery, the painstaking needlework: Great-aunt Amelia's yearly gift of love to, and for, us.

Custom...is the great guide of human life.
–DAVID HUME

CHRISTMAS EVE GIFT

DEE ANN PALMER

On December 24th, the phone rang in my home in California.

"Hello," I said.

"Christmas Eve gift!" came a voice all the way from Fort Worth, Texas.

"Oh, Aunt Butis, you caught me! You win!" I cried.

Christmas Eve gift! Christmas Eve gift! Childhood memories came flooding back. This was a game unique to our family. Somewhere my grandmother had learned of a family tradition where the first one to call out that phrase on the appropriate day to other family members received a gift from them.

The trick, and the fun, of course, came in catching the others off guard, in being the one to sing it out first and win the gift.

Grandmother's family was too poor to give gifts, and so they played the game for fun. Mother had initiated my sister, Kay, and me into the rites of the tradition. Kay, being ten years older, usually won. The day came, however, when she had been out late the night before and I was awake early with anticipation. I crept into her still-dark room, pounced on her, and yelled, "Christmas Eve gift!" at the top of my lungs. Thereafter it was a more even match.

That was the Christmas I asked Mother, "How come we don't give gifts?" It occurred to me that the game would be greatly improved by such an addition.

"Oh, we get plenty of those," Mother replied. "But this is the special gift. This one won't be broken by December 26th, and nobody, including big sisters, can coax it away from you. It's the gift that lasts a lifetime. You see, the gift we get is *love*."

She smiled and hugged me, but I was a child and was disappointed with her answer. I was old enough, however, to understand that it was one for which there was no argument.

Even after Kay and I were grown and married, we continued to play the game. But then Mother died one September. Shocked and grieving, we had no sense of delight with which to play that year. The tradition died, forgotten until today. Now my Mother's sister greeted me with it, and I felt a gentle warmth.

When our call was over, I put the receiver back and thought of all the years my family had touched each other with those words. Then I picked up the phone again and placed a call to my father.

"Christmas Eve gift, Daddy!" I sang out.

In the brief silence that followed, I knew that his memories had also been stirred. Pleasure filled his voice when he finally answered.

"I love you, too, Sugar," my daddy said. "Christmas Eve gift!"

The warmth spread and filled me. Once again the special gift was mine.

We do not remember days, we remember moments.
—CESARE PAVESE

MY MOST MEMORABLE CHRISTMAS

CATHERINE MARSHALL

hy is one Christmas more memorable than another? It seldom has anything to do with material gifts. In fact, poor circumstances often bring out the creativity in a family.

But I think the most memorable Christmases are tied in somehow with family milestones: reunions, separations, births, and yes, even death. Perhaps that is why Christmas, 1960, stands out so vividly in my memory.

We spent that Christmas at Evergreen Farm in Lincoln, Virginia—the home of my parents. With us were my sister and her husband—Emmy and Harlow Hoskins—and their two girls, Lynn and Winifred. It meant a typical family occasion with our three children, Linda, Chester, and Jeffrey, along with Peter John, who was then a senior at Yale. Five children can make an old farmhouse ring with the yuletide spirit.

For our Christmas Eve service, Lynn and Linda had prepared an improvised altar before the living room fireplace. Jeffrey and Winifred (the youngest grandchildren) lighted all the candles. Then, with all of his family gathered around him, my father read Luke's incomparable account of the first Christmas. There was carol singing, with Chester and Winifred singing a duet, "Hark, the Herald Angels Sing," in their high piping voices. Then my mother, the storyteller of the family, gave us an old favorite, "Why the Chimes

Rang." She made us see the ragged little boy creeping up that long cathedral aisle and slipping his gift onto the altar.

Then she said, "You know, I'd like to make a suggestion to the family. The floor underneath the tree in the den is piled high with gifts we're giving to one another. But we're celebrating Christ's birthday, not each other's. This is His time of year. What are we going to give to Jesus?"

The room began to hum with voices comparing notes. But Mother went on, "Let's think about it for a few moments. Then we'll go around the circle and each of us will tell what gift he or she will lay on the altar for Christ's birthday."

Chester, age seven, crept close to his father for a whispered consultation. Then he said shyly, "What I'd like to give Jesus this year is not to lose my temper anymore."

Jeffrey, age four, who had been slow in night training, was delightfully specific: "I'll give Him my diapers."

Winifred said softly that she was going to give Jesus good grades in school. Len's was, "To be a better father, which means a gift of more patience."

And so it went on around the group. Peter John's was short but significant. "What I want to give to Christ is a more dedicated life." I was to remember that statement five years later at the moment of his ordination into the Presbyterian ministry when he stood so straight and so tall and answered so resoundingly, "I do so believe...I do so promise...." Yet at Christmastime, 1960, the ministry was probably the last thing he expected to get into.

Then it was my father's turn. "I certainly don't want to inject too solemn a note into this," he said, "but somehow I know that this is the last Christmas I'll be sitting in this room with my family gathered around me like this."

We gasped and protested, but he would not be stopped. "No, I so much want to say this. I've had a most wonderful life. Long, long ago I gave my life to Christ. Though I've tried to serve Him, I've failed Him often. But He has blessed me with great riches—especially my family. I want to say this while you're all here. I may not have another chance. Even after I go on into the next life, I'll still be with you. And, of course, I'll be waiting for each one of you there."

There was love in his brown eyes—and tears in ours. No one said anything for a moment. Time seemed to stand still in the quiet room. Firelight and candlelight played on the children's faces as they looked at their grandfather, trying to grasp what he was saying. The fragrance of balsam and cedar was in the air. The old windowpanes reflected back the red glow of Christmas lights.

Father did leave this world four months later—on May 1. His passing was like a benediction. It happened one afternoon as he sat quietly in a chair in the little village post office, talking to some of his friends. His heart just stopped beating. That Christmas Eve he had known with a strange sureness that the time was close.

Every time I think of Father now, I can see that scene in the living room—like a jewel of a moment set in the ordinary moments that make up our days. For that brief time, real values came clearly into focus: Father's gratitude for life; Mother's strong faith, my husband's quiet strength; my son's inner yearning momentarily shining through blurred youthful ambitions; the eager faces of children groping toward understanding and truth; the reality of the love of God as our thoughts focused on Him whose birth we were commemorating.

It was my most memorable Christmas.

*Miracles are instantaneous; they cannot be summoned,
but they come of themselves, usually at unlikely moments
and to those who expect them.*

—KATHERINE A. PORTER

SANTA'S HELPERS

ELSA BONSTEIN

On Christmas Eve, my husband and I awoke to the sound of early morning cartoons. Our grandsons, Timmy and Danny, were downstairs, where our daughter and son-in-law were preparing breakfast. They'd sold their starter house and would be staying at our home in New Jersey until they found something bigger. We were thrilled to have the whole family together for the holidays.

There was one sticking point, though. Three-year-old Timmy was worried that Santa wouldn't be able to find him. "Our house is your house for now, Timmy," I'd told him while we baked cookies the day before. "Santa knows where you live." But the sad look didn't leave his eyes. Danny, two, picked up on his big brother's mood, and soon both of them were moping around the house. Christmas Eve morning I lay in bed listening for the boys downstairs, hoping to hear them laugh. Lord, how can I assure them they won't be overlooked?

I'd read them the Christmas story! After all, the wise men had searched and found the baby Jesus. Perfect, I thought. I climbed out of bed, ready to show my grandsons some Christmas spirit.

"Reindeer ! Reindeer! Hurry,"Timmy called from downstairs.

We all ran to the picture window in the living room. There on the front lawn was a herd of deer. They stood in a clump and stared back at us. Eventually they lost interest in our amazed faces and made their way into the woods. As they moved across the lawn, we counted. Six big-eyed does accompanied by two fawns, one peeking out from behind its mother, made eight all together. Timmy looked at me and smiled. "Santa sent his eight reindeer to find us," he said.

Danny broke into a broad smile. "Santa!" he cried.

We couldn't remember the last time we'd seen one deer, much less a whole herd, near our house. Ever since the surrounding area had been developed, deer sightings had been extremely rare. God had beat me to the punch once again. Before I could help my grandsons find some Christmas spirit, Christmas had found them. "Come, boys," I said, "I want to read you a story."

*It is easier to be wise on behalf of others
than to be so for ourselves.*
—LA ROCHEFOUCAULD

GRAMMY'S CRÈCHE

ELAINE ST. JOHNS

The Grammy who started it all was my mother, Adela Rogers St. Johns. It was after I moved to California with my two-year-old daughter, Kristen, and six-year-old son, George. We all lived together, along with an aunt and uncle and various friends and relations, in a family compound called *The Hill*.

As Christmas approached, Grammy decided more than one Christmas tree was redundant, so for her house she bought, instead, a sturdy, rustic, peak-roofed shed, charming Mary and Joseph figurines, a small wooden manger, and of course the Royal Infant Himself. The whole was set up on a living room table surrounded with holiday greens and poinsettias (the Infant hidden snugly out of sight until Christmas Eve). The children thought the very merry Christmas tree at our house was "pretty"; but at Grammy's house, where we gathered together on Christmas Eve, and Baby Jesus appeared in the manger, Grammy's crèche, though simple, was the focus of reverence and awe.

Small wonder that Kristen and George started to save from their pocket money to add to Grammy's crèche. On those long-ago Christmas Eves, as we read the Christmas story from the Gospels, the children would present their gifts. One year an exotic Wise Man; another, four tiny shepherds and one too-large sheep; then a blue ceramic donkey; a plump porcelain angel with a rose atop her head...

The children grew up, married, and moved away. Grammy's work as a writer led her to move permanently to a hotel in New York. *The Hill* was no more, and the crèche went into storage.

Then my granddaughter was born. It was just before Jessica's first Christmas that a large package was delivered to me from the storage warehouse. The card read, "From one grandmother to another." It was Grammy's crèche. And there they were—Mary and Joseph and Jesus, the Wise Man, the big sheep and too-small shepherds, the blue donkey minus one ear, the angel sans rose, but what matter? I carefully set the scene on a table in the living room. After all, more than one Christmas tree is redundant!

It was before this manger that Jessica and later her brother Bogart learned the blessed Christmas story and the beloved carols. And then these two began to bring gifts to the stable. An early offering was a tiny gift-wrapped package of peanuts. Later, with allowances hoarded throughout December, Christmas by Christmas, arrived a variety of angels, several deer, a cow, and more odd sheep. Not quite every beast of the field nor all the great sea monsters gathered before the Holy Family, but there did appear a white horse, an otter, a lion, a handsome orangutan, Jonah's whale, and, since Bo found out what Behemoth meant, a hippopotamus.

Grammy's crèche became a neighborhood attraction, with all the children dropping by each year during Christmas week to watch it grow.

Two years ago, Jessica and Bo made an Advent wreath to place at the manger site, and each of the four Sundays before Christmas we ceremoniously lighted a candle and sang carols. This past year they arranged the scene themselves, using my brick fireplace with its raised hearth. Books, stacked to form a series of gentle terraces to the hearth, were covered with a white sheet and cotton snow, sure footing for men and beasts. The fireplace was filled with pine boughs from their yard, and on the hearth itself was the crèche with its familiar, well-loved figures.

On Christmas Eve, as Jessica, now ten, placed the Infant in His manger and as her mother, father, Bo, and I sang one last "Silent Night," I inwardly thanked my mom for her gift. Not only for the tangible objects themselves, but for her gift of wisdom in establishing a tradition that strengthens our family and its sense of continuity. For one day, I know, in the not-too-distant future, I will give my daughter Grammy's crèche: "From one grandmother to another."

Help your brother's boat across, and your own
will reach the shore.

—HINDU PROVERB

OUR "OUT-OF-THE-BLUE" CHRISTMAS

DORIS C. CRANDALL

It was Christmas Eve, 1933. Mama was preparing to bake her "hard-times fruit cake," so called because the only similarity to fruit it contained was prunes. To our family, however, it was an extra-special cake. My sisters, Lottie, Vivian, Estelle, and Dolly, and I sat around our kitchen table shelling pecans for the cake.

None of us, except Mama, was enthusiastic, and I suspected her gaiety was partly put on. "Mama," I asked, "why can't Grandma and Aunt Ella, and Aunt Fran and Uncle Hugh, and all the cousins come for Christmas like last year? We won't even have any music unless Joe comes and brings his guitar."

We wouldn't miss not having a Christmas tree because we'd never had one, and Mama and Daddy had prepared us for the possibility of no presents, but the thought of no visitors or music really subdued our spirits. Dolly, aged five and the youngest, sobbed.

"Why'd we have to move, anyway?" she asked, sniffing. So Mama again explained her version of dust-bowl economics.

"When we had to give up our farm we were lucky to find this place to rent, even if it is too far for the relatives to come. Don't worry, though," Mama reassured us. "Why, God might send us company for Christmas right out of the blue if we believe strong enough." She began to mash and remove the pits from the boiled prunes.

As we worked, a wind came up and whistled through the newspaper we'd stuffed into the cracks in the corners. A cold gust blasted us as Daddy entered through the back door after doing the chores at the barn. "It looks like we're in for a blue norther," he said, rubbing his hands together.

Later, Daddy built up a roaring cow chip and mesquite fire in the pot-bellied stove in the living room, and we were about to get into our flannel nightgowns when someone knocked on the door. A traveler, wrapped in his bedroll, had missed the main road and stopped to ask for shelter from the storm for the night.

"Mind you," he said, when he'd warmed himself and had a cup of hot coffee, "I don't take charity. I work for my keep. I'm headed for California. Heard there's work to be had there."

Then Mama fixed our visitor a cozy pallet behind the stove. We girls went into our bedroom and all crawled into the same bed for warmth. "Reckon he's the one Mama said God might send out of the blue for Jesus' birthday?" I whispered. Dolly yawned.

"I'm too young to know," she said.

"He must be. Who else'd be out in weather like this?" Lottie said, and Vivian and Estelle agreed. We snuggled, pondered, and slept.

At breakfast our guest sopped biscuits and gravy. "I never had a family that I remember," he said. "Can't recollect any name 'cept Gibson. You can call me Mr. Gibson if you want." He smiled, revealing gums without teeth. Seemingly, he had no possessions beyond his bedroll and the clothes he wore, but he pulled a large harmonica from his pants pocket and said, "I've always had this. Want me to play something?"

So Mr. Gibson spent Christmas Day with us, and what a delight he was. He helped with the work, told us stories, and played all the beloved Christmas songs on his harmonica. He played by ear as we sang church hymns. After much pleading on our part, he agreed to stay one more night.

The next morning, when we awakened, Mr. Gibson was gone. I found his harmonica on the kitchen table. "Oh, Mama," I cried, "Mr. Gibson forgot his harmonica—the only thing he had." Mama looked thoughtful.

"No," she said softly. She picked it up and ran her palm over the curly-cues etched in the metal sides. "I think he left it on purpose."

"Oh, I see," I said, "sort of a Christmas present. And we didn't give him anything."

"Yes, we did, honey. We gave him a family for Christmas," she said, and smiled.

We never saw Mr. Gibson again. Daddy had an ear for music and quickly learned to play the harmonica. Through the years it brought many a joyful memory of that unforgettable Christmas—the Christmas when God sent us Mr. Gibson right out of the blue—a blue norther, that is, because He knew how much a man with music, who longed for a family, and a family without music, who longed for company, needed each other.

Music, the greatest good that mortals know,
and all of heaven we have below.

—JOSEPH ADDISON

THE CHRISTMAS CONCERT

MARGARET PEALE EVERETT

Three years ago, on December 24th, a special invitation appeared at each of our places at breakfast. It was made of half a piece of construction paper, folded over, with a tiny ribbon poked through holes in one corner. On the front, in bold magic marker, it read: YOU ARE CORDIALLY INVITED...

Our children, Jennifer, age eleven, and Chris, age eight, eagerly flipped theirs open and then looked disappointed. As I opened mine, seeing my husband's familiar handwriting, I read:

... to a special candlelight concert of recorded Christmas music from 4:30 - 5:30 P.M. December 24. R.S.V.P.

"What's this all about?" I asked Paul.

"You'll see."

"But I don't have time to sit for an hour listening to music tonight. We have to eat an early dinner, be at church at 7:30, and I still have presents to wrap and..."

"You don't have to come," he interrupted. "Just R. S. V. P. 'no.' I will be there, and I'd love to have any of you join me who want to."

The children said 'no' immediately, but I said nothing, deciding to leave it on the back burner of my mind during the day.

At 4:30, frankly, I'd forgotten the invitation. I had just dashed in from a last-minute errand when I noticed that Paul was lighting all the candles on the first floor of our house.

"What are you doing?"

"It's time for the concert."

Paul flipped on the stereo and the music began. The beautiful sounds of Christmas filled our home. One song after another, from the *Messiah* to "Joy to the World," from choir to solo to instrumental engulfed me, and I finally stopped my activity and joined Paul in the living room. There we watched the flickering candles send shadows of dancing light all over the room, our bodies and souls quieted by the music proclaiming Christ's birth.

We have now received three such invitations. This past Christmas our daughter, now fourteen, listened from the family room, our son from the kitchen. This year my parents visited us. As they opened their invitations, I could "read" their thoughts: "I can't sit for an hour listening to music." However, when 4:30 arrived, they joined us—just to be polite, I'm sure! For one hour we sat still and let the timeless music of Christmas infuse our thoughts and quiet our hearts. And as they left us for the airport two days later, my father said, "I'll never forget that wonderful hour of music. I really felt the spirit of God preparing me to celebrate Christmas."

These days we talk a lot about remembering the spirit of Christmas, but for me, at least, it is still too easy to get all caught up in things to do and places to go. Now I have at least one hour-on December 24th—which brings me back to the heart of Christmas and gives us a chance to meditate on the importance of Christ's birth to us.

When you see the value of continued growth, the circumstances around you become stepping stones.

−CLYDE M. NARRIMORE

THE TIE CLIP

RICHARD H. SCHNEIDER

It was the day after Christmas, 1932, and a blustery wind traced white veins of snow across the sidewalk in front of our house. I glanced out the window of our living room where I was playing with my Christmas toys and the joy of the moment was snuffed as quickly as a candle.

Uncle Emil was coming.

A black sheep in the family, he worked on and off for the Chicago and Northwestern Railroad. He held the job only because he had lost an arm as a youngster while ducking between some freight cars, and the railroad felt it owed him this much.

However, the loss never seemed to bother Uncle Emil. Often, when his heavy jowls were flushed, he would take a stance like an angry bull elephant in the middle of the living room and boast of how many men he had fought to the ground with his one good arm. Every once in a while he would disappear into the bathroom and reappear ruddier than ever. It took me a few years to realize that it wasn't his kidneys but a pocket flask that prompted these frequent visits.

He had been married once, or twice; no one really knew. And now he lived alone in a room on Chicago's west side.

Uncle Emil talked incessantly of things of no interest to a ten-year-old: of ways to win at the race track, important positions he had turned down at the railroad, and, after several trips to the bathroom, of new speakeasies he had found. Bored almost to sleep, I listened only with half an ear.

One unforgettable year when his voice reached a high intensity, he became quite enthused about a new set of false teeth. Suddenly he took them out and flung them across the room for me to inspect. Trying to hide my disgust, I gingerly handed them back and ate little dinner afterwards.

Thus, every December as the holiday approached, I would complain to my mother about Uncle Emil's impending visit. "But why, Mom, why?"

"Because it is Christmas."

"He ruins Christmas."

"He has nowhere else to go," said Mother, her mouth firm, signaling an end to the discussion.

And now Uncle Emil was coming. Two days ago, Mother had given me a dollar to buy a gift for him.

As I entered the five-and-ten, a seed of evil entered my soul. Looking at the worn dollar bill, I could see no reason why I should buy that man a gift when there were so many things I needed. There was a model of the Gee Bee Sportster airplane I had always wanted to build. It cost seventy-five cents, but I could still find something nice for Uncle Emil with the remaining quarter.

Finding something for twenty-five cents wasn't as simple as I had thought. But the salesgirls were beginning to drape clothes over the counters as closing time neared, and I settled on a cheap gold-colored tie clip.

I eased my conscience with the thought that, after all, he never brought us a Christmas present. At least an aunt brought chocolate coins in gold foil, though they tasted of moth balls from a year's storage in her dresser drawer. She always bought her holiday gifts at after-Christmas markdowns.

Uncle Emil settled himself in his usual chair, and again I sat through the usual harangue, interspersed with bathroom breaks.

I had not shown Mother his gift. I wrapped it beforehand and presented it to Uncle Emil in the living room while Mother added last-minute touches to the dessert. Just as he unwrapped it, Mother stepped into the living room. One glance at the tie clip and she turned to me, eyes blazing. Then, quickly covering her anger, she said: "Come, Emil, it's time for dinner."

Heaving his ponderous bulk from the cushioned chair, he slipped the tie clip into a coat pocket and lumbered to the table.

After dinner, Mother helped him into his coat and then stood at the living room window watching him walk, head bent into the swirling snow, to catch the streetcar.

Retribution rained heavily on me that night. Mother informed me in no uncertain terms that Uncle Emil never wore ties because he couldn't knot them. And, if I had any thought for others, I could see that.

The following spring Uncle Emil died. After the funeral, Mother and I went to clean out his room, a small, dingy chamber that smelled of mouthwash and shaving soap, with a cracked green shade at the window. It was the first time that I saw where he lived.

While Mother packed clothes into a carton for the Salvation Army, I studied the walls of his room. Cracked yellowing snapshots were stuck inside the frame of his mirror; here and there an old letter, wrapped in a ribbon. Treasured fragments of those he had loved. And then something caught my eye. I couldn't believe it. Up on the wall, clipped on a Christmas card from our family was the cheap tie clip, tarnished by the past four months.

On the card with it were some words in his labored scrawl. I stood on tiptoe and dimly made them out:

"Christmas, 1932, from my nephew."

Suddenly, Uncle Emil's life fell in on me—his losing battle with the world, his hunger for companionship, his longing to have someone with whom to talk.

The shadowed glint of the tie clip wavered and dimmed in my vision. Wiping my eyes, I moved over to Mother, stumbling gently into her side.

"Mom," I said over a lump swelling in my throat, "I'm awfully glad we had him for Christmas."

She glanced up at the tie clip, and then at me. She reached down and gripped my shoulder for a moment. I think she knew that in Uncle Emil's room I had begun to grow up.

God gave us memory that we might have roses in December.
—SIR JAMES M. BARRIE

OUR LIGHT IN THE NIGHT

MARGARET PEGRAM MORRISON

When I was a child, there was always an evening in late November when Daddy would say to Momma, "What do you think? Sunday after this one coming up is the first Sunday of Advent. Isn't it time to start our star?"

Without waiting for an answer, all three of us children would jump up to clear the dishes. Daddy would put the extra leaf in the table, and Momma would get out white paper, cardboard patterns, and the blunt-end scissors. It was time to make our Moravian star.

We lived in Winston-Salem, North Carolina, and because the town of Salem was first settled by members of the Moravian church, we celebrated many of their customs. In their churches the Moravian stars were hung, but we made one for our own front porch.

Every night for a week the scene after supper was the same. We traced the patterns and cut, folded, and glued until we had finished all of the star's twenty-six fragile points. Sometimes Daddy read the Christmas story as we worked. Sometimes he talked about how the wise men of today still need a light to guide them. Momma helped when a fold went crooked and wiped up sticky smudges where small hands put more paste on the table than on the paper.

Making each point was tedious work. The seams were so small it was hard for us to get them folded straight. When one of the points was misshapen, Momma or Daddy asked, "Would you feel better if you did it over?" We children would decide whether the point was worthy of going onto the star. And each night the row of points placed on the sideboard to dry grew longer.

One evening when we were nearing the end, my little sister called, "Finished! Finished!" But then she bumped the table with the very last point and crushed it as she was taking it over to dry. She began to cry, but Momma took over, bending the point until it began to straighten. Then Brother exclaimed, "We have to cut one anyway to put in the light. That point can be the one that lights the star!"

The smile that Momma and Daddy exchanged lit the room.

Daddy had rigged a socket on a short electrical cord. The broken end of the point was cut off and the cord threaded through. Then we all went out to the front porch and watched proudly as Daddy hung the star and turned on the light. And what a glorious light it was. As a matter of fact, when placed inside the Christmas star, the same bulb that the rest of the year was just bright enough to light our way up the porch steps was so brilliant it was visible more than a block away.

Perhaps grown-up hands patched up our work after we had gone to bed. Perhaps those same hands repaired joints in the star when they came loose. All I know is that year after year, whether there was snow or sleet, that fragile creation made of white paper and flour-and-water paste lasted from the first Sunday of Advent to Epiphany. No matter how wide it swung in the night wind, it was whole and still shining the next morning.

Nowadays the stars are made of durable plastic and are available in kits.

Each year when I hang my sturdy holiday star, I close my eyes and see the stars of my childhood. I picture us gathered around them to declare this year's creation the best one ever!

And I still hear Momma and Daddy as they prayed that each of us might strive to be worthy so that the light of the star could say, "You will find God present here."

A friend in need is a friend indeed.
—ENGLISH PROVERB

A TRADITION ALL HER OWN

FRANCES E. WILSON

Carefully she placed the small figure of the Christ Child in the crèche. For seventeen years, setting up the crèche just before Christmas had been her special tradition. As she stood back to admire it, she recalled the year it came to her. Yes, came to her with warmth and love...

She was ten years old that first Christmas of the crèche. It was just two weeks before the big day and all the houses on Mulberry Street were decorated with wreaths of green fir and bright red ribbons.

Pamela started counting them as she walked home through the powdery snow that had frosted the town white the night before. She noticed that even old Mrs. Kessel had hung a wreath on her door. It must have taken a lot of effort, Pamela thought, for she was badly crippled with arthritis and could barely get about.

Pamela lifted her feet in high steps and continued marching along. She made a path of big holes as she pushed her feet squarely down into the drifts of fresh snow. She hoped it would snow some more. You need to have snow for Christmas, she thought. Just like you need to have those Christmas customs her teacher had talked about at school that day. Miss Snyder had told the class about the special things people did to celebrate the holidays: putting lights and tinsel on the Christmas tree, wreaths of pine cones, hanging stockings, caroling. Pamela did wish, however, that she had something special she could do at Christmas, a custom all her very own. She thought about that as she walked the rest of the way home.

Once inside the warm house, Pamela hung up her coat and hurried into the kitchen where her mother was chopping nuts and measuring candied fruits for fruitcakes. Pam took a round, red apple from a bowl on the kitchen counter and bit into it. She watched her mother pour the nuts and fruits into a glass mixing bowl.

"Mother, you always make fruitcakes for Christmas, don't you?" she asked, her elbows propped on the counter top, her eyes studying her mother.

"Yes, I guess you'd say that," her mother answered, stirring the mixture with a wooden spoon. "In fact, fruitcake and floating island pudding are holiday traditions I've known since I was a girl, even younger than you. Some time you could learn to make it; then you'd be carrying on a family tradition."

"I guess so," Pam sighed, tossing her apple core in the trash bin. "What I'd really like, though, is a tradition all my own. Dad always picks out the Christmas tree for us and sets it up in the tree stand. Tommy always puts the lights on the tree because he's tall enough to reach all the branches. Why, even Annie gets to place the silver spire on the top of the tree, and she's just a baby!" Pam sighed and pushed her brown hair back behind her ears.

Her mother put her arm around Pam's shoulders and gave her a quick hug. "Your daddy used to hold you up to put the silver ornament on top of the tree. Don't you remember that? That's always been the special job for the youngest member of the family."

"That's just it! Everybody in our family has something special to do for Christmas!" Pam bit the corner of her lip. "Everybody but me!"

"You could string cranberries and popcorn to hang on the tree," her mother said.

"That would be O.K. for one time, I guess," Pam said with a shrug. "But I want something more." She narrowed her eyes thoughtfully. "I want something that could really make Christmas special for me, too— every year."

The next day after school Pam walked with slow steps toward home. Her head bent down, she shuffled her feet through the snow. "I just don't feel much like celebrating Christmas this year," she said half aloud. As she reached down to scoop up a handful of snow, she caught sight of a folded newspaper sunk in a pillow of snow at the edge of Mrs. Kessel's yard.

Grabbing the paper, she hurried up the walk and rang the doorbell. She brushed the snow from the paper with her mittens as she waited. She knew it would take Mrs. Kessel a while to answer the door, for she walked very slowly using a cane.

"Pamela, my dear," the grey-haired lady greeted her with a smile of welcome. "My newspaper, how nice of you, dear. Won't you come in and visit with me? It's too cold to stand out there." She smiled at Pamela.

Entering Mrs. Kessel's living room, Pam stuffed her mittens in her coat pocket and took a seat on the couch near Mrs. Kessel's rocking chair. She did like visiting Mrs. Kessel. She was always so friendly, and everyone in the neighborhood liked to listen to her stories. And she was a good listener, too. Pam found she was soon telling Mrs. Kessel all about her wish to have a special Christmas custom, telling her about Mother's special pudding and how Anne was the one who put the top spire on the tree.

"You know, Pam, I believe I have something put away that will interest you," Mrs. Kessel said as she leaned forward in her rocker and pointed toward the dining room. "Go open the right hand door of the buffet and bring me the white, cardboard box you'll find there."

In a minute Pam returned with a box tied with white string. "What is it? What's in this box?" she asked. She was finding this an exciting mystery, and her fingers trembled as she worked to untie the string.

"You'll soon see, dear," Mrs. Kessel said with a smile.

With a gentle yank, Pam had the cord free. Lifting the box lid, she discovered several packages wrapped in tissue paper.

"Take each of them out, one at a time," Mrs. Kessel instructed. "As you unwrap them you can set them in order here on the rug." She pointed to the space in front of her chair.

Pam had already begun pulling away the tissue. "Oh, what a darling little wooden lamb!" she exclaimed as she put the small carved animal on the rug and reached again into the box.

Within a few minutes, she had four more sheep and three long-legged camels lined up on the carpet. She opened a larger package and discovered it contained several shepherds and also three kings. Pam knew they were kings, because they wore crowns on their heads.

"Why, these are the shepherds who took care of all the lambs and the kings who rode on their camels to see the Baby Jesus," Pam cried, her voice filled with delight. "It's just like the manger scene in front of our church!"

"That's right, Pamela. It's called a crèche. At Christmas time in my home in Vienna my family always placed these nativity figures and the manger on the mantle above our fireplace."

"This was your special custom then, wasn't it?"

Mrs. Kessel nodded. "I haven't set it up for several years now. It is so difficult with my arthritis, you know."

"I'll set it up for you!" said Pamela excitedly. She placed the rustic crib on Mrs. Kessel's mantle and arranged the kings and the shepherds, Mary and Joseph. Carefully she took the tiny figure of the Christ Child and placed it gently in the crib.

"Thank you, my dear," said Mrs. Kessel. "But now I'm afraid you'll have to come back after Christmas and pack them away."

"Oh, I don't mind," said Pamela. "I'll do it very carefully. And next year ... next year, I'll set them up for you again. I mean—could I, Mrs. Kessel?" Pamela ran to the woman and knelt at her feet, her face bright with anticipation.

"Yes, yes, Pamela, I'll look forward to it," said Mrs. Kessel. "Our little visits mean so much to me."

Suddenly Pamela struck her forehead with the palm of her hand. "This is it," she cried. "My very own Christmas tradition!"

For five more years, Pamela set up and took down Mrs. Kessel's crèche at Christmas time, sharing with the elderly woman moments of peace, warmth, and friendship. When Mrs. Kessel died, her will stipulated that the crèche should go to Pamela.

Now she stood in her living room, staring at the lovely figures with wonder that filled her every year at this time. As she touched them, her two-year-old toddled in from the playroom.

"What's that, Mommy?"

She picked him up and held him close. "That's Mommy's very own tradition," she said.

He looked puzzled. "Someday you'll understand," she murmured.

That best portion of a good man's life: his little, nameless, unremembered acts of kindness and of love.

—WILLIAM WORDSWORTH

A STRAW-FILLED CHRISTMAS TRADITION

LYNNE LAUKHUF

It all began a few years ago. It was several weeks before Christmas, and our family was busy preparing for the holiday. Excitement was everywhere. Our two children, Adam, aged three, and Shannon, aged eight, delighted in baking and frosting the Christmas cookies; I was running around doing errands and Christmas shopping; and my husband, Larry, was out searching for the perfect tree. The traditional wreath had gone up on the front door, and inside the house, candles, holly, and a garland completed the festive look.

But one afternoon, following a long day of baking and gift-wrapping, I walked into the living room, sank into the sofa, and propped my tired feet on the coffee table. The excitement of the holiday had turned to exhaustion and the joy of the season was fading. Where in all of these preparations, I wondered, is the message that Christ has come into the world? Our family was so busy preparing for Christmas that perhaps we'd lost sight of its true meaning.

That evening I told Larry about my concern. "How can we put Christ into our Christmas?" I asked him. He seemed to agree with me that materialism had taken hold in our house and we ought to get our attention back to the spiritual—Christ's coming.

No, we didn't decree an end to our Christmas festivities, but we did add a preparation that was to become meaningful to all of us. We took our manger scene and placed it in a prominent place in the dining room. As usual, the children carefully unpacked the plaster of paris figures that had been saved from my husband's childhood and placed them around the manger.

However, we left the infant crib empty. Next to the manger we placed a small bowl filled with pieces of straw. Since all children understand that babies need a soft, comfortable bed in which to lie, we explained that we had to get ready for the Baby Jesus to come and that we would fill His crib with bits of straw.

Then we told them about the most important part of this new family tradition. "Giving gifts at Christmas is a message of love," Larry explained. "You can give gifts to the Baby Jesus, too." The children's faces lit up.

"That's right," I picked up. "We won't give Him presents wrapped in ribbons and bows, but we can do kind and loving things for others, in His name. And each and every time we do a kindness for someone else, we will put a piece of straw in the empty crib. By Christmas we'll have our special gift for the Baby Jesus." The little ones nodded and beamed with excitement. They were eager to begin.

During those weeks before Christmas, a special anticipation was added to our home. Small deeds of kindness were secretly performed and the bed was slowly filling ...

One afternoon when I came home, the dirty breakfast dishes had been washed and cleared from the dishwasher. After a snow-filled day of sledding, Adam (with a little help from his dad) had secretly put away Shannon's sled for the night. A call from Nana told us of the special hand-drawn pictures the children had sent in the Christmas mail. And one morning, we awoke to find two round, shining faces awaiting us with "breakfast in bed"—a bowl filled with milk and a few spoonfuls of cereal.

So it went. I even discovered my son's little playmate quietly slipping into the house to put in a few bits of straw. Little surprises never ceased, and the manger was looking quite comfortable with its thick bed of hay.

On Christmas morning the crib was full and Shannon carefully placed the Baby in His love-filled bed. After breakfast we gathered around the manger with a specially baked birthday cake and sang "Happy Birthday to Jesus."

Each year when we repeat this family tradition it becomes more special. And as we sing to Him on Christmas morning, we remember it is His day after all, and that we have prepared ourselves for His coming and have given Him many fine gifts of love.

Love & Blessings

Appearances often are deceiving.
—AESOP

BLESSED ARE THOSE IN THE LOBBY

RICHARD CRENNA

When I was growing up, a typical Christmas morning was spent quietly having breakfast with my parents in a local restaurant. Resting on the table would be the gift my folks had just presented me after the waitress took our order.

Of course I was happy, but it wasn't like racing downstairs in your own house in the morning to find a present under the tree.

We always ate out because we lived in the Stephens, a hotel in downtown Los Angeles. The seventy-two-room residential hotel was owned by my parents. It was during the Depression, and Mother managed it to supplement Dad's income as a pharmacist. Growing up in the city had its benefits. I loved riding streetcars, took my first communion at nearby Precious Blood church, and attended a local school with Asian, Latino, and black kids. Though I was a minority, we kids were never aware of differences; we were friends. All in all, I considered myself privileged.

But, Christmas in a hotel always had a downside, for I never had a real *family* Christmas. Friends told me of houses, fragrant with roasting turkey, and of relatives gathering around the tree in the living room. Since Mom, Dad, and I lived in only two rooms, *our* tree always went up in the hotel lobby. So I never had anything to brag about. With me it was always, "Here comes Christmas again, and I've got to go down and wish a happy holiday to all those sad-eyed people in the lobby." For the Stephens was full of unfortunates who spent Christmas alone.

Some were characters straight from Damon Runyon stories: gamblers, con men, bookies, and former jockeys. Others were right out of Ripley's Believe It or Not! Like the Most Tattooed Man, who was our night clerk. His real name was Ted Rockwell, and his body was covered with tattoos of his name, in every language, as well as in Chinese pictographs, Morse code, and signal flags.

Then there was the World's Greatest Thief, who, it was said, had walked out the front door of Abercrombie & Fitch in New York City with a canoe and then went back the next day for the paddles. An elderly silver-haired man, he had already paid his debt to society.

Our *femme fatale*, Mae Taylor, who had lived at the Stephens for more than twenty years, fancied herself a movie star. Then there was Tumbleweed, who looked just like his name when he came down the street after a night out. He bounced from side to side off buildings before rolling his way into the hotel. One night while we were all sitting around the big Atwater Kent radio in the lobby, somebody dropped him inside the door, saying, "I think this belongs to you."

Mom helped him up to his room and tucked him into bed. She was a mother figure to all our seventy-two guests, though she made sure none of the bookies or gamblers plied their trade in the hotel. The only time I saw her angry was the night a lady checked in and within fifteen minutes had hung a red light bulb over her transom. Mother put her out immediately.

In my young mind, I disdained these people as has-beens and losers. And I often took advantage of their foibles. The Germ Man had a phobia about bacteria and always wore a face mask. When meeting him on the stairs, I'd take great delight in sneezing as loudly as I could and as many times as possible. He'd bolt madly for his room and Mother would scold me for my unkind behavior.

Watching this strange assortment of people, I believe, actually started me on my acting career. I used to mimic the things they did, especially the drunks. At an early age I could fall down a flight of stairs without hurting myself. I must have rolled into the Stephens's lobby a thousand times.

It was only natural for me to take drama at Virgil Junior High. The CBS and NBC radio studios were nearby, and a friend and I fished through their garbage bins for discarded scripts. We used them to stage our own plays, adding some imaginative sound effects.

One day while we played football on the playground, our drama teacher came out and said, "Boys, they're auditioning for a new radio program at station KFI. I want you all to try out. It will be good experience."

Dirty and sweaty, we traipsed over to KFI to audition for a program called *Boy Scout Jamboree*. It was a comedy about a troop of nine Scouts who did everything wrong. A group of us were hired for twenty-five cents a Saturday show, and I ended up staying on the program for many years. I played Herman, a prototype of all the other goofy, adenoidal, adolescent kids I later portrayed on *The Great Gildersleeve, The Hardy Family,* and *One Man's Family*.

This led to my being considered for the role of Henry Aldrich on *The Aldrich Family* radio series. Another actor, Dickie Jones, and I were asked to go to New York City to audition in January 1942. As a sixteen-year-old, I was thrilled to be going all the way across the country, even though I knew only one of us would get the part.

But I wasn't expecting what happened that Christmas Eve. Mother and Dad ushered me into the pine-scented lobby, where I saw all the residents gathered around the tree. The hand-cranked Victrola was screeching out Christmas carols.

It was a surprise Christmas celebration and going-away party for me. I was stunned. Each resident had a gift for me. I had no idea that they really cared. Mae Taylor presented me with monogrammed handkerchiefs in a fancy box. Tumbleweed, cold-sober for a change, handed me a pocketknife with all kinds of built-in tools. The World's Greatest Thief, his skyblue eyes shining, gestured to the floor. There sat an expensive set of matched Hartmann leather luggage.

"When you go to New York, Dick," he said, "you've got to look successful." I glanced at Mom apprehensively. But she smiled and pointed to the zippered canvas covers with my name stitched on them. The World's Greatest Thief had purchased this luggage—for me.

Even the Germ Man and the drunks I had relentlessly mimicked offered me their congratulations. I remembered my old priest saying that if you "bless them that curse you… ye shall be the children of the Highest" (Luke 6:28, 35). I hadn't actually cursed any of these people, but I certainly had made fun of them. And now they were paying me back with kindness and encouragement. Sad-eyed people in the lobby? Well, here I was, misty-eyed at their loving support. It was now clear. The men and women I had once written off as has-beens and weirdos were instead children of the Highest.

For the first time, I began to see that people are equal. And I understood Mother's compassion for former thieves, gamblers, and bookies. You love people for what they are, not for what you wish them to be.

Soon I was on the train toward New York with my father, who had taken time off to chaperon me. A fellow passenger finished exclaiming about his own holiday, then turned to me. "And how about you?" he asked.

I leaned back and smiled. "It was my best Christmas ever," I said. "I spent it with. . . my family."

Light is the task when many share the toil.

—HOMER

MOTHER HELPED ME DO IT

DRUE DUKE

The pungent fragrance of the decorated pine tree filled the house, hanging especially heavy in the kitchen's warm air. Soon the fruitcake I had put into the oven would add its spicy smell.

I slipped the mixing bowl and measuring cup into the dishwasher and checked my list on the counter.

"Cheese straws next," I said aloud.

I had a lot to do in preparing for our annual Christmas open house. But the last thing I needed in my compact kitchen was a pair of eighty-five-year-old hands.

Yet, there she was, at my elbow, asking her persistent question, "What can I do to help you?"

I felt my jaw tighten against the words I didn't want to say. Mother knew that we were delighted to have her come for a visit over Christmas with us. She knew, too, of my long-standing determination that she would do no work while in my home. One of God's basic commandments is to honor one's father and mother, and there was no greater dishonor I could do her than to shove my chores off on her.

"Why don't you go into the den and enjoy television?" I managed to ask patiently.

"There's nothing good on now." She leaned against a base cabinet, exactly where I needed to get. "It's some story I don't understand."

I knew she had difficulty hearing at times and couldn't always unravel the plots on TV. And since she was alone all day while I was at work, she probably was lonesome to be with me. A quick surge of love and tenderness for her made me say gently, "I'll pull a dining room chair out here and you can sit and talk to me. How's that?"

From the chair that I placed out of my way she watched me line up ingredients along the counter.

"I'll grate the cheese for you," she volunteered brightly.

"Now, Mother, that arthritis in your hands..."

"Honey!" she cut in so sharply I turned to look at her. "This arthritis," holding up a wrinkled hand, "doesn't hurt nearly so badly as just being useless."

"Oh, Mother!" The hunk of cheese banged on the counter as I let it go to slip an arm about her. "You are not useless!"

"I may be old," she said stoutly, "but there are some things I can still do."

"Of course there are." I turned back to the counter, clearing a place. "Such as grating cheese. Right?"

We smiled at each other and she stood up, ready to get busy. I put a high stool up to the counter. She could not get up on the seat, but she propped against it long enough to grate the cheese. While she worked, she chatted brightly about two sisters who always brought cheese straws to the senior citizens' meetings back home in Georgia.

"I think I'll sit down a bit," she said when the cheese was a mound of golden shreds.

From the corner of my eye I could see her hands shaking. I knew she was tired, but her flushed face was beaming. Her talking had caused me to forget how much flour I had measured, and I had to redo it.

But as I measured, I realized there was something far more wrong than my need to redo: my attitude. How foolish I had been. I brought her into my home but had not made her a part of it. I had treated her like an ornament that was nice but not necessary. I called my actions "honoring," when in reality they were hurting. I hadn't looked closely enough to see her need to be needed.

"I plan to do the salted nuts tomorrow night," I said in a quick decision. "But I haven't shelled the pecans. If I crack them tonight, will you pick them out for me tomorrow?"

"Of course I will." She rocked forward on the chair, stretching toward me. "Anything I can do to help you, just tell me."

My mind searched and found another request.

"You know that arrangement with the red candles that I made for the mantle?" I asked. "I'm not satisfied with it. I wish you would help me remake it."

As my hands moved through the heavy dough, mixing flour and water and cheese, she watched and made small talk. A smile played about her lips, and I realized I was wearing one to match it. It was a precious moment for both of us, one I knew how to keep.

In days to come I'd ask her to fold some towels from the dryer, to stamp envelopes for Christmas cards, to lay out silver on the party table—all tasks she could handle. If the results were less than perfect, what difference would it make?

And when our guests commented on a lovely party, how proud we both would be that I could say, "Mother helped me do it!"

The only gift is a portion of thyself.
—RALPH WALDO EMERSON

THE GIFT THAT LASTS A LIFETIME

PEARL S. BUCK

He woke suddenly and completely. It was four o'clock, the hour at which his father had always called him to get up and help with the milking. Strange how the habits of his youth still clung to him after fifty years! He had trained himself to turn over and go to sleep, but this morning, because it was Christmas, he did not try to sleep.

Yet what was the magic of Christmas now? His childhood and youth were long past, his father and mother were dead, and his own children were grown up and gone. He and his wife were alone.

Yesterday she had said, "Let's not trim the tree until tomorrow, Robert. I'm tired."

He had agreed, and the tree was still out in the yard.

He slipped back in time, as he did so easily nowadays. He was fifteen years old and still on his father's farm. He loved his father. He had not known how much until one day a few days before Christmas, when he had overheard what his father was saying to his mother.

"Mary, I hate to call Rob in the mornings. He's growing so fast and he needs his sleep. I wish I could manage alone."

"Well, you can't, Adam." His mother's voice was brisk.

"I know," his father said slowly, "but I sure do hate to wake him."

When he heard these words, something in him woke: his father loved him! He had never thought of it before. He got up quicker after that, stumbling blind with sleep, and pulled on his clothes, his eyes tight shut, but he got up.

And then on the night before Christmas, that year when he was fifteen, he lay on his side and looked out of his attic window. He wished he had a better present for his father than a ten-cent store tie.

The stars were bright outside, and one star in particular was so bright that he wondered if it really were the Star of Bethlehem. "Dad," he had once asked, "what is a stable?"

"It's just a barn," his father had replied, "like ours."

Then Jesus had been born in a barn, and to a barn the shepherds and the Wise Men had come, bringing their Christmas gifts.

The thought struck him like a silver dagger. Why should he not give his father a special gift? He could get up early, earlier than four o'clock, and he could creep into the barn and get all the milking done. He'd do it alone— milk and clean up, and then when his father went in to start the milking, he'd see it all done. And he would know who had done it.

He must have waked twenty times during the night. At a quarter to three he got up and put on his clothes. He crept downstairs, careful of the creaky boards, and let himself out. A big star hung low over the barn roof, a reddish gold. The cows looked at him, sleepy and surprised.

He had never milked all alone before, but it seemed almost easy. He kept thinking about his father's surprise. He smiled and milked steadily, two strong streams rushing into the pail, frothing and fragrant. The cows were still surprised but acquiescent. For once they were behaving well, as though they knew it was Christmas.

The task went more easily than he had ever known it to before. Milking for once was not a chore. It was something else, a gift to his father who loved him.

Back in his room he had only a minute to pull off his clothes in the darkness and jump into bed, for he heard his father up. He put the covers over his head to silence his quick breathing. The door opened.

"Rob!" his father called. "We have to get up, son, even if it is Christmas."

"Aw-right," he said sleepily.

"I'll go on out," his father said. "I'll get things started."

The door closed and he lay still, laughing to himself. The minutes were endless—ten, fifteen, he did not know how many—and he heard his father's footsteps again.

"Rob!"

"Yes, Dad."

"You son of a-" His father was laughing, a queer sobbing sort of a laugh. "Thought you'd fool me, did you?"

"It's for Christmas, Dad!"

His father sat on the bed and clutched him in a great hug. It was dark and they could not see each other's faces.

"Son, I thank you. Nobody ever did a nicer thing."

"Oh, Dad." He did not know what to say. His heart was bursting with love.

"Well, I reckon I can go back to bed," his father said after a moment. "No, listen—the little ones are waking up. Come to think of it, son, I've never seen you children when you first saw the Christmas tree. I was always in the barn. Come on!"

He got up and pulled on his clothes again and they went down to the Christmas tree, and soon the sun was creeping up to where the star had been. Oh, what a Christmas, and how his heart had nearly burst again with shyness and pride as his father told his mother and made the younger children listen about how he, Rob, had woken up all by himself.

"The best Christmas gift I have ever had, and I'll remember it, son, every year on Christmas morning, so long as I live..."

They had both remembered it, and now that his father was dead he remembered it alone: that blessed Christmas dawn when, alone with the cows in the barn, he had made his first gift of true love.

On an impulse, he got up out of bed and put on his slippers and bathrobe and went softly upstairs to the attic and found the box of Christmas-tree decorations. He took them downstairs into the living room. Then he brought in the tree. It was a little one—they had not had a big tree since the children went away—but he set it in the holder and put it in the middle of the long table under the window. Then carefully he began to trim it.

It was done very soon, the time passing as quickly as it had that morning long ago in the barn. He went to his library and fetched the little box that contained his special gift to his wife, a star of diamonds, not large but dainty in design. He tied the gift on the tree and then stood back. It was pretty, very pretty, and she would be surprised.

But he was not satisfied. He wanted to tell her—to tell her how much he loved her. It had been a long time since he had really told her, although he loved her in a very special way, much more than he ever had when they were young.

Ah, that was the true joy of life, the ability to love! He was quite sure that some people were genuinely unable to love anyone. But love was alive in him, alive because long ago it had been born in him when he knew his father loved him. That was it: love alone could waken love.

And he could give the gift again and again. This morning, this blessed Christmas morning, he would give it to his beloved wife. He could write it down in a letter for her to read and keep forever. He went to his desk and began his love letter to his wife: My dearest love ...

Then he put out the light and went tiptoeing up the stairs. The star in the sky was gone, and the first rays of the sun were gleaming in the sky. Such a happy, happy Christmas!

*Adversity not only draws people together, but brings forth
that beautiful inward friendship.*
—SOREN KIERKEGAARD

BECAUSE OF A BABY

MARY BLAIR IMMEL

A don't think Christmas is ever going to come," I said, staring moodily out of the window.

"Why, it's only a little over three weeks away," Mother said.

"I don't mean that. I mean it's not going to seem at all like Christmas this year."

We had lived in Southern California for eight months now, and the mild weather gave us no clue as to the season. We had to consult the calendar to remind us that it was the first week of December.

From where I sat I could see lush green lawns instead of grass a winter-kill brown. Rather than maples reaching bare branches against a mottled gray Kansas sky, I saw palm trees with accordion-pleated fronds on a background of cerulean. Inside there were no familiar pots of impatiens rescued from frost to bloom on the windowsills. Instead we looked out on exotic gardens replete with bird-of-paradise and lily of the Nile.

So much about our life here in San Diego seemed uncomfortably strange to us. Our small utilitarian apartment in the garish pink stuccoed building bore no resemblance to our weather-beaten old frame house back in the flatlands where we had a commodious kitchen and a maze of rooms upstairs and down.

Most disturbing of all was the fact that we didn't really know many people out here. I had a few friends, but I seldom saw them except at school. Back in Kansas we knew everyone in town. Somebody was always popping in our back door with a jar of home-canned piccalilli or a fruitcake made from someone's great-grandmother's recipe.

Here, we were cheek by jowl with the folks in the next apartment, but the only neighbors' names we knew were those printed on the twenty mail slots in the first floor lobby. What's worse, we couldn't match any of those names with the faces we occasionally saw in the hallway.

Like so many others of that time, our family had moved west hoping to find steady employment. My father felt lucky to get a job as a guard at one of the aircraft factories. But even having work that brought in a regular paycheck didn't make up for the feelings of displacement that we were experiencing. We often prefaced our sentences with the words, "When we go back to Kansas . . ."

Of course, it wasn't all bad. Even though the California winter wasn't our idea of what Christmas weather ought to be, it was fun to be able to astound aunts and uncles back in the Middle West when we wrote letters describing the unusual aspects of our life out here. They couldn't imagine our having a picnic in winter, but that's exactly what we were doing on that first Sunday of December 1941.

It wasn't the kind of fried-chicken-and-angel-food-cake picnic we had been accustomed to back home. This Sunday, right after church, we had gone to Old Town for tamales. Those steaming delicacies, wrapped in corn husks, were placed on trays, which we carried outside. We sat to eat at long trestle tables beneath lacy-leafed pepper trees.

We had only just started to eat when someone called out, "Here's another bulletin coming in about Pearl Harbor."

I'd never heard of Pearl Harbor, but then, geography wasn't my best subject in school. It took us a few moments for the awful news to sink in. We left our trays and gathered around a radio. We listened, stunned, as details of the attack were repeated.

Although we had lived for the past months in a city where soldiers and sailors and marines crowded the streets alongside aircraft factory workers, the thought of actually being at war seemed unreal.

That afternoon my father left the apartment for work at the plant, where he was on the swing shift from three until midnight.

Mother and I stayed close to our table radio. That evening we listened to news reports instead of the "Jack Benny Show."

Just before it was time for me to go to bed, there was a faint knock at our apartment door. I went to answer and was surprised to see a small boy staring up at me.

"My mother's sick," he said and reached for my hand.

Mother followed us along the hallway and into a studio apartment. A single unshaded bulb lit the sparsely furnished room. Along one wall were two canvas cots.

A little girl of two, wide-eyed and obviously frightened, sat on one of the cots. The mother of the children lay groaning on the other.

"The baby's too early," the young woman cried out. "Help me, please."

Mother knelt by the cot and talked comfortingly to the moaning woman as I hurried to find a telephone to call an ambulance.

I knocked on five different doors until I found someone who had a telephone. By the time the young woman was taken to the hospital, the occupants of most of the other apartments on our floor had gathered in the hallway to see what was happening.

"Where's her husband?" asked a man whose Oklahoma tones reminded me of those of my uncle who lived in Ponca City.

"She told me that he's stationed aboard a ship at Pearl Harbor," Mother said. "He was supposed to get leave when the baby was born, but I guess today has changed all that. The poor girl doesn't even know if he's alive."

Mother repeated the story of how young Evie Gibson and her two little children had come to San Diego on a bus from Colorado. She had run out of money because her husband's allotment checks had not caught up with her. Probably it was the news about Pearl Harbor and the worry about her husband that had started labor six weeks early.

"Well, we'd best get these two young'uns bedded down," said a neighbor with a soft Kentucky drawl. "We've got room at our place."

The neighbors moved slowly back to their own apartments, but I sensed in all of us a reluctance to leave the crowded hallway. It was as though we had some unfinished business to attend to.

Early the next morning the woman from the apartment across from ours came over with freshly baked breakfast rolls.

"My name is Hallie," she said. "I come from Wymore, Nebraska."

"Come in, Hallie," Mother invited, and she seemed to savor being on a first-name basis with a neighbor. "Sit down and have a cup of coffee."

"Have you heard anything about Evie Gibson?" Hallie asked.

Mother shook her head, but added, "My husband and I are going to the hospital today to let her know that Johnny and Sally are being well cared for. We'll let you know what we find out."

When I got home from school that afternoon, I learned that Evie had given birth to a four-pound baby boy. Mother spread the word to all our neighbors.

"He's cute as a button," Mother said. "But he's so tiny and Evie is so anemic that the doctor is going to keep both of them in the hospital for a couple of weeks."

Papa contacted the Red Cross and learned that Seaman First Class John Gibson was safe and would be told about his new son.

It was Hallie who came up with the idea about the Gibsons' apartment. "If Evie is going to be in the hospital for two weeks, that will give us time to do something about that terrible place she lives in."

"I've got an extra lamp with a shade that would brighten up that room," said Arla Mae of the soft Kentucky drawl.

"The walls need a couple of coats of paint first," said Sam, who had come from Oklahoma looking for work as a carpenter.

"That new baby can't sleep on a cot," said Shirley in her practical Hoosier manner. "I'll bet Cecil and I can find a crib at a secondhand store."

"We have a Boston rocker we don't use much anymore," offered Lucretia.

So it was that almost everyone in that apartment house thought of some way to make a contribution to the project. The Gibson apartment became the center of activity around the clock. Day-shift people painted walls during the evening. Those on the graveyard shift spent their afternoons trimming woodwork. Swingshift workers scraped paint off windows at odd hours in between.

Little by little, that horrid room where Mama and I had first seen Evie and her two children began to take on a homey atmosphere. Furnishings seemed to materialize out of thin air. Shortly after Shirley and Cecil bought a secondhand crib, beds appeared for Evie and the children. Then someone moved in a bedside table. The next day a lamp was put on the table. Before long there was a crocheted doily under the lamp and a small ceramic figurine. Even a couple of framed watercolor prints found their way onto the freshly painted walls. Hallie and Mama, Lucretia, Shirley, and Arla Mae worked together for days making patchwork comforters for the beds, exchanging a lot of their own family histories as they talked and sewed.

The day Evie and the baby came home from the hospital, Papa bought two Christmas trees, one for us and one for the Gibsons. We showed Johnny and Sally how to string popcorn and cranberries. To this day I can smell the white library paste we smeared on colored construction paper to make the chains that we looped over the dark green branches. Better still, I can remember vividly the sound of laughter as all of us neighbors gathered to admire the baby and leave gifts under the Gibsons' tree. We stayed to sing carols, and for the first time since we left Kansas, Papa got out his fiddle and played, while Sam accompanied him on the harmonica.

I wonder how many of us realized what had happened to us because a baby was born. No longer were we strangers in a strange place. In a way, we had all come home. And Christmas had come after all.

Friendship is the only cement that will ever hold the world together.
−WOODROW WILSON

MY VERY SPECIAL CHRISTMAS TREE

MADELINE WEATHERFORD

Christmas was the most special holiday of all for my father. The preparations, gift buying, and decorations were no trouble to him and just added to his overall enjoyment.

I was introduced to my first Christmas tree when I was nine days old. Mother told me that it was a small tree, but every ornament, candle, and piece of silver tinsel were meticulously hung in place, as only my father could do it. When he had finished, he took me from my bassinet and held me up to see his handiwork.

There were to be just four more of Daddy's Christmas trees—each one a little larger than the year before. And, of course, as I grew older his delight in Christmas rubbed off on me and it became my favorite holiday, too.

However, this year was going to be different. A short bout with pneumonia in February had snuffed out Daddy's life.

As Christmas drew near, Mother sat down with me and as gently as she could explained, "Madeline, we won't be able to have a tree and decorations this year because we're in mourning."

"In mourning" meant nothing to a four-going-on-five-year-old little girl. I missed my wonderful daddy and my once gay and beautiful mother, now weighed down by her grief.

Christmas Eve arrived with no special arrangements for the next day, other than early Mass and dinner with relatives. In the afternoon the phone rang and Mother answered.

"Oh, hello, Mrs. Dreyfus," she said. And after a pause, "That's very kind, but I think we'll spend the evening here together. It's the first since—" She recovered and thanked Mrs. Dreyfus again and hung up.

Mrs. Dreyfus was one of several Jewish families who lived in our apartment house. They had been wonderful to Mother in helping her meet her sorrow and adjust to widowhood.

"What did she want?" I asked.

"She wanted us to come down this evening. I—can't."

"Oh, please, Mother," I cried. "She always has hot cocoa for me."

Mother was silent most of the day, and later in the evening she changed her mind. She called Mrs. Dreyfus and told her we'd stop in for a few minutes. "It's kind of her," Mother said, "and thank goodness they won't have any Christmas decorations."

We rang the doorbell and Mrs. Dreyfus welcomed us into the foyer. The living room beyond seemed dark with an odd-colored glow.

She led us into the living room, where we were greeted with cries of "Merry Christmas." Seated around a beautifully decorated Christmas tree were Mrs. Abrams, Mrs. Cohen, and Mrs. Blount. Under the tree were gaily decorated packages for us. And Mrs. Dreyfus didn't disappoint me. There was cocoa for me and coffee for the ladies.

There have been many trees since then—big, small, fresh, and artificial— but I always think of that one as my very special Christmas tree. I'll never forget those loving, caring people who shared in an unfamiliar custom so that one little girl without a daddy could have a Merry Christmas.

Today I can close my eyes and bring back that scene at will. Many times it has sustained me when things have gone badly, for I can still feel the warmth and love of those neighbors. It taught me the true meaning of Christmas—the brotherhood of man.

Sorrow looks back, worry looks around, faith looks up.
—GUIDEPOSTS

THE DIME STORE ANGEL

BARBARA ESTELLE SHEPHERD

When our twin daughters were toddlers and Scotty was still a baby, my husband, Dick, and I dug into our meager Christmas fund to buy a dime store angel for the top of our tree. Aesthetically, she was no prize: the plastic wings were lopsided, the gaudy robes painted haphazardly, the reds splashing over into the blues and purples. At night, though, she underwent a mysterious change—the light glowing from inside her robes softened the colors and her golden hair shone with the aura of a halo.

For six years she had the place of honor at the top of our tree. For six years, as in most families, Christmas was a time to be especially grateful for the wonderful gifts of God.

And then, in the seventh year, as summer enfolded us in her warm lethargy, I became aware of a new life gently stirring beneath my heart. Of all God's gifts this seemed the culmination, for we had long prayed for another child. I came home from the doctor's office and plunged straight into plans for a mood-setting dinner.

That evening when Dick walked in, candles flickered on the table and the children took their places, self-conscious in Sunday clothes "when it's just Wednesday!"

"Oh-oh," he grinned, "Mother's up to something—one of those special dinners again." I smiled and waited till halfway through the meal to make the announcement. But I got no further than the first informative sentence.

"You mean we're gonna have a baby?" squealed Miriam. Milk overturned and chairs clattered. Doors slammed and Dick and I were alone with our happiness while our three small Paul Reveres galloped wildly over the neighborhood shouting their news to everyone within lung distance.

Summer and fall sped by as we turned the spare room into a nursery and scraped and repainted baby furniture. December came again; once more we were on the verge of Christmas. Then one morning, eight weeks too soon for our new nursery to be occupied, I was rushed to the hospital.

Shortly past noon our four-pound son was born. Still groggy from the anesthetic, I was wheeled—bed and all—to the nursery to view Kirk Steven through an incubator porthole. Dick silently squeezed my hand while we absorbed the doctor's account of the dangers Kirk would have to overcome in order to survive. Added to his prematurity was the urgency for a complete blood exchange to offset Rh problems.

All that long afternoon Dick and I prayed desperately that our son's life be spared. It was evening when I awoke from an uneasy doze to find our minister standing by the bed. No word was spoken, but as he clasped my hand, I knew. Our little boy had lived less than twelve hours.

During the rest of that week in the hospital, grief and disbelief swept over me by turn. At last Dick came to take me home. He loaded my arms with a huge bouquet of red roses, but flowers can never fill arms that ache to hold a baby.

In the street outside I was astonished to see signs of Christmas everywhere: the decorated stores, the hurrying shoppers, the lights strung from every lamppost. I had forgotten the season. For the sake of the children at home, we agreed, we would go through the motions. But it would be no more than that.

And so a few days later Dick bought a tree, and mechanically I joined him and the children in draping tinsel and hanging glass balls from the branches. Last of all, on the very top, went the forlorn dime store angel. Then Dick flipped the switch and again she was beautiful. Scotty gazed upward for a moment, then said softly, "Daddy, this year we have a real angel, don't we? The one God gave us."

And Dick and I, in our poverty, were going to give Christmas to our children—forgetting that it is always we who receive it from them! For, of course, God was the reality in tragedy as He had been in our joys, the unchanging joy at the heart of all things. Scotty's words were for me like the light streaming now from the plastic angel, transforming what was poor and ugly on the surface into glory.

*What do we live for if not to make life
less difficult for each other?*
—GEORGE ELIOT

THE RED MITTENS

ROSALYN HART FINCH

Christmas was coming and I was doing some heavy complaining to Mama about pocket money. "All the other kids in fifth grade are gonna buy their Christmas gifts," I said pointedly when Mama suggested that "home-made gifts are more love-filled than bought ones."

"How come we always have to be poor?" I grumbled.

"Being poor has nothing to do with giving," said Mama. "It's not what you give, but how you give."

But I didn't agree.

Christmas week was unseasonably warm for Ohio, turning the month-long layers of snow into messy puddles and slush. But things began looking up for me; I had an idea.

Early on Saturday morning I bundled up my five-year-old brother, Dicky, who owned the one and only wagon on the block, jammed my way into my mackinaw, shoved on boots and gloves, emptied the wagon of Dicky's junk, and took off with Dicky in it.

Across the backyard and through the stubbled cornfield that edged along the rear of our property and spread as far as our eyes could see, I trotted, pulling Dicky and the wagon behind me.

The wagon wheels fitted neatly in between the rows of stubble, but pulling Dicky through the half-thawed slush was rough. I was so fired up with enthusiasm for my plan, however, that I scarcely noticed.

At last, reaching the train tracks bordering the cornfield, I unfolded my plan to Dicky.

"What we're gonna do, Dicky, is load the wagon with all the hunks of coal we can find beside the tracks. Then we'll take it to the gas station and sell it. A girl in my class says her cousin does it all the time. We're lucky the snow's mostly melted or we couldn't see it."

"For money?" Dicky's eyes widened. "Will I get some, too?"

"Sure," I promised. "We both will."

"Oh, boy." Dicky scuttled out of the wagon, eager to begin. "How'd this stuff get here?" he asked, stooping to brush the remaining slush from a chunk of "black gold."

"It falls off the trains," I cried happily, tossing chunks into the wagon as fast as I could pick them up. I'd never dreamed there'd be so much.

In short order we had stacked a small black mountain and were headed toward the gas station, Dicky pushing and me pulling. By the time we'd reached the road to the station, Dicky was whining and crying, filled with cold and fatigue.

An old woman I'd often seen at church, Mrs. Scott, was out sweeping the slush from her front porch. "What's wrong, children?" she called.

"Nothing," I yelled back. "My brother's just cold."

"Why don't you bring him inside by the stove? I could fix you both some hot cocoa."

Dicky ran to the offered haven. Much as I'd have loved a little warmth and some cocoa, I declined. I was anxious to get the money the coal would bring me. I left Dicky and said I'd be back.

Puffing and blowing, I trudged the lead-heavy load the rest of the way alone. My numb feet were stumbling at everything and my fingers burned. My heart hit bottom when the gas station man said, "Didn't cha' notice the weather's turned? We ain't buying any more coal. We're full up."

Tears of disappointment stung my eyes as I grabbed the wagon handle and ran back, tears streaming down my face. How I arrived at Mrs. Scott's house again I don't recall.

"Dicky has to go home now," I managed to say, looking down at the ground.

"Whatever's the matter, dear?" Mrs. Scott said, drawing me gently inside and wiping my tear-stained face with her apron. "Come by the kitchen stove for some cocoa."

Dicky pulled my sleeve. "Didja get the money? Didja get the money?" he jabbered, holding out a ready hand.

That did it. My misery broke loose and I sobbed out my disappointment. "There isn't any money. The gas station man wouldn't buy the coal."

Dicky hugged my knees in silent commiseration.

When I lifted my head to wipe my tears, Mrs. Scott held out a steaming cup of cocoa. "What a shame, dear. Dicky told me how hard you both worked."

I nodded. "I was counting on it for a Christmas present for my class exchange."

Mrs. Scott kept shaking her head, clucking sympathetically. Then her concerned face brightened. She hurried over to the cupboard, reached up to the top shelf, and lifted down an ancient yellowing teapot. Pulling off the lid, she dumped out a dollar bill, a dime, and a nickel.

"Would this be enough to buy your coal?" she asked, spreading it out on the table.

Money! My eyes fairly leapt at the sight of it there, then lingered on Mrs. Scott's hands as they smoothed out the dollar bill. They were red and rough. I raised my eyes and for the first time noticed the patch on her apron and the faded kitchen curtains and the newspaper taped to the windows.

My heart sank. *She couldn't really spare the money for the coal.*

A pile of bright red mittens sat on the countertop. I looked at them curiously. "I just knitted those for our missionary society," she said. "Here, try a pair." They were much too big for me, but I didn't let on.

"They're beautiful," I said, for they were. "I bet anyone would love to have them." Staring at the money on the table, I suddenly knew what to say. "I'll trade you the coal for a pair of mittens, Mrs. Scott."

"Would you really like them?" asked Mrs. Scott. I nodded.

"I think we've made a fine exchange," she beamed as she pulled her sweater about her shoulders. It was chilly away from the stove....

Well, I ended up giving one of Mama's "homemade gifts" for my class gift-exchange that year, and I kept Mrs. Scott's snug red mittens for myself. Her gift warmed my hands all winter long; and more importantly, my heart was warmed whenever I thought of my gift of coal to her.

Mama was right. Love-filled gifts are the best. Mrs. Scott and I had made a fine exchange.

Life is not always what one wants it to be, but to make the best of it, as it is, is the only way of being happy.

—JENNIE JEROME CHURCHILL

MY PERFECT CINDERELLA DOLL

MADGE HARRAH

The sidewalk was bustling with shoppers as my mother and I hurried to the department store. I craned my neck for a peek at the holiday window display, but at six I was too small to see around the grown-ups with their winter coats and packages. When at last we reached the store, I stood transfixed. "Look, Mother," I whispered, pressing my hands against the glass. "Cinderella."

Before my eyes was the most beautiful doll I had ever seen! She wore a fairy princess gown with layer upon layer of glittering pink tulle. I knew if I lifted the hem of her skirt I would find glass slippers. The tiny tiara fastened to her silky golden hair sparkled, reflecting the Christmas lights. If only she were mine, I dreamed. We'd have tea parties and share secrets and waltz with a handsome prince. My mother steered me away from the window, explaining that she and my father could not afford such an expensive doll. "But there will be a very special gift under the tree for you on Christmas morning, Madge," she said. "I promise."

Later that week I leaned against Mother's sewing machine, watching the needle flash up and down. "Bet you don't know what this is!" she teased, holding up the cloth for me to inspect.

"My Christmas doll!" I squealed. It was still in the early stages, but I could make out the head, neck, and body. I knew she would soon be soft and beautiful, just like the doll at the store.

"So much for my surprise!" Mother laughed as I twirled around the room, already pretending Cinderella and I were at the ball. It wouldn't be long now.

My excitement grew with each passing day. Mother continued to work on the doll, and whenever I walked into the room she would hide it under a pillowcase. I could tell by her smile that she was pleased with her progress.

On Christmas morning I jumped out of bed and tore down the hall toward the living room. At the doorway, though, I stopped. There, underneath the tree, was a doll. Her black yarn hair was pulled back in a tight knot. She had a plain, handstitched face. And she wore a simple, boring plaid dress. She wasn't Cinderella; she looked more like the ugly stepsister.

But I could see Mother watching me, an eager look on her face. I wondered how she must be feeling. Mother worked hard on this doll, I thought. If I don't like it, she'll be sad.

Trying to hide my disappointment, I rushed across the room, shouting, "I love her, I love her!" Then I buried my face in the doll's skirts and silently prayed: God, please help me like her. I stood there for a long moment and heard my mother's startled intake of breath, followed by a pleased laugh.

For the rest of the day, I made myself carry that homely doll everywhere. I even "fed" her part of my Christmas dinner. "Oh, Madge," Mom said at one point, "I'm so glad you like her!"

"Her name is Patsy," I replied. It was no use calling her Cinderella.

In the weeks that followed I kept up my act. Patsy went everywhere with me. When I was sick, she shared my pillow. When I was lonely, Patsy kept me company. A strange thing happened. Soon it wasn't an act at all.

Even after Cinderella arrived the next Christmas, Patsy remained my closest companion. Her black yarn hair pulled loose and waggled about her face, but I sewed it back in place. When holes appeared in her cloth body I darned each one. Her plaid dress pulled open at the seams, so I made her an elaborate ball gown, complete with a crown. A princess at last! But to me, Patsy was already perfect. All she had needed to become beautiful was a little girl's love. Simple, enduring, transforming love. It was a real Cinderella story after all.

There is no such thing as chance; and what seems to us the merest accident springs from the deepest source of destiny.
—JOHANN VON SCHILLER

HOLIDAY CANDLES

BETTY GIRLING

The most memorable Christmas in my life occurred many years ago when I was eleven. My father and mother had left Ohio to homestead in Nebraska. Our first winter there began bleak and cold and, above all, lonely. We had no neighbors. Once there'd been other homesteaders nearby, but they'd moved before we came. Across the fields their cabin stood empty.

In Ohio we'd been used to friends and activity and going to church; but here we lived too far out, and my father made the long trip into town only occasionally for supplies.

A few days before Christmas, Pa saddled our horse, Thunder, and rode off to town to get the candles he'd promised for our tree.

Shortly after he left, Mother and I were surprised to see a team of horses approaching the empty farmhouse across the field. Soon we could see figures unloading furniture.

"Neighbors!" Mother cried joyfully.

The next moment she had on her coat and was trudging across our snow-crusted cornfields with a loaf of fresh baked bread. Soon Mother was back, accompanied by a girl of my age.

"This is Sarah Goodman," she said.

Sarah and I looked at each other shyly. Then I found myself telling her all about the Christmas tree we were going to have when Pa got back from town.

Softly, Sarah said to me, "We're Jewish."

I'd never known a Jewish girl before. Suddenly I felt silly, babbling about trees and candles, and I was sorry for Sarah, not having any Christmas.

"Well, never mind," I told her, struck by a sudden thought. "You have special holidays too, I guess."

"Oh, yes, we have Hanukkah," she began eagerly. "That's our Feast of Lights . . . " She broke off and jumped to her feet. "Oh, with all the moving, we've forgotten! Why, it's already. . . " she counted on her fingers, "it's the fifth day. And I don't even know where we packed the Menorah!" Then with a hasty good-bye she ran out and across the fields to her own house.

Mother and I watched her go in surprise, wondering what a "Menorah" might be. Even as we watched, it began to snow.

I stayed at the window all afternoon, peering into the white maelstrom. Faster and thicker the snow fell—till I couldn't see Mother's lilac bush a scarce five feet away.

At six o'clock Pa had not returned, and Mother's face was grim. Here on the plains *blizzard* is a fearsome word. Hadn't they told us in town about the homesteader they found last winter, frozen to death only four feet from his own barn door?

At 11:00, when Mother finally put me to bed, the blizzard was still raging and Pa had not returned.

At dawn the storm was over. Deep snowdrifts piled high around the house, but the sky was clearing. Mother was sitting in a chair, still waiting. Suddenly we heard shouts and raced to the door.

Pushing through the drifts came my father, Sarah Goodman, and her parents. In they tramped. Soon we were all clustered around the kitchen stove, getting warm.

"It was a miracle," Pa said. "That's what it was, a miracle."

While Mother cooked breakfast, Pa told us how he'd been lost in the storm. The road was completely obliterated, he could see nothing in the dark, and he had to depend on the horse's instinct for guidance. But finally Thunder wouldn't go on.

"I was nearly frozen by then," Pa said. "So I jumped off the horse and started leading him, just to keep warm. For hours we floundered on. We'd work one way till the drifts got too deep, then turn and work another."

Pa knew he was pretty close to exhaustion when suddenly, through the swirling snow off to one side, he saw some tiny pinpoints of light.

"As I led Thunder toward those lights, I prayed they would still keep shining, and when I reached them I found myself at the Goodmans' cabin. There in the window was a great candlestick, like none I'd ever seen before. Nine candles it held, six of them lighted."

"That was our Menorah," said Sarah, "for Hanukkah, our Feast of Lights. I put it in the window."

"Then you saved Pa's life!" I said.

"Not exactly," said Mr. Goodman gently. "Sarah really put it on the windowsill hoping you would see it and know that she was celebrating her holiday, at this time, like you will be keeping your Christmas."

Mother set us down to breakfast just then, and Pa bowed his head, saying: "Almighty God, we thank Thee for the blessings of this season."

Generosity lies less in giving much than in giving at the right moment.
—JEAN DE LA BRUYÈRE

LOVE APPLE

COLLEEN GRAHAM

The first snow of the season had dusted the amber leaves that cold Wednesday morning in Bozeman, Montana. Fall seemed to be my busiest season. A widow with four grown children, I had gone to seminary in my late forties and was in my first assignment, pastoring two small country churches. I loved my work, but as the days became shorter and the temperature plunged, I felt my energy flag and a quiet creep into my soul. I lifted my eyes from my cluttered desk to look out the window at snow-covered Bridger Peak, longing for the warm sunshine of spring.

Just then my office door opened. Marion Brown, our church pianist, greeted me with a cheery hello. She shook the snow from her black boots and unbuttoned her heavy ankle-length coat. Smiling impishly, she put her hand in her pocket and took out a large apple. "This is for you," she said, thrusting it toward me. "To bring some color into your life."

"Thank you so much," I said. It was a perfect Red Delicious, so shiny I could see my reflection in its ruby surface. "Where did you find such a beauty?"

"A salesman going north gave it to me this morning. He wanted to thank me for playing his favorite songs last night." Marion and her invalid husband lived in the local hotel, and she often played the piano in the lobby.

"Stay for a minute and warm up," I said, gesturing to the chair next to my desk.

"No, I'm off to a Kiwanis Club meeting to wake them up with some lively music." She laughed. "Then I'll be playing at the hospital later on." At one time or another every organization in town took advantage of Marion's musical gifts. "I've got to go."

"Thanks again," I called after her, then put the apple on my desk.

My first appointment of the day turned out to be a serious one. Steve, a college student and part-time logger, looked grave as he sat down, taking off his cowboy hat.

"It's Lucy," he said. Lucy, his sister, was in the hospital, expecting her first child.

"What's happened?" I asked.

"She's afraid she might lose the baby." He twisted his hat in his lap. "I'm scared. I know how much this means to her and her husband. To all of us…"

I assured him God was caring for his sister and her baby. Then we prayed. As he rose to go, his eyes fixed on the apple. "Is that real?" he asked.

"Yes," I said. And then I was struck by an urge to give it away. "Take it."

"I couldn't," he protested.

"You must," I insisted. "Take it to your sister. Give it to her as a reminder that God is looking out for her. Tell her you prayed for her."

"Thanks," he said. He picked up the apple and hurried out.

The day continued with a flurry of activity. By sundown I was ready to head home. As I sat in my car waiting for it to warm up, I saw a familiar silhouette making her way through the snow. I rolled down my window. "Marion! Marion!" I called. "Need a ride?"

She crossed the street, shifting the bags she carried. "No, thanks," she said. "I like the exercise. But I've got to tell you about my day." She swung open the car door and eased in beside me, brushing back her dark hair.

"You know how I play at the maternity ward of the hospital every Wednesday?" I nodded. "Well, when I'm done I visit each new expectant mother for a few minutes. Today the nurses alerted me to one young girl who was having some problems.

"Her name was Lucy, and she confessed she had been feeling low. Then her brother made a surprise visit. He brought her a big red apple—just like the one I gave you this morning."

I smiled.

"He told her it was a special apple and it would remind her God was with her. She laughed out loud when she said that, and at the same time the baby inside her jumped. That was just what she'd been praying for. You'll never guess what happened next."

"What?" I asked.

"She handed me the apple, saying, 'I want you to have it.'"

"How wonderful!" I exclaimed, biting my tongue.

"It's even more perfect than the one I gave you this morning," she said.

My husband will be so pleased. He hasn't been feeling well lately, and I know this will cheer him up."

The apple had completed its circle. As they say, gifts travel far in the hands of giving people.

True religion. . . is giving and finding one's happiness by bringing happiness into the lives of others.
—WILLIAM J. H. BOETKER

THE MAGIC CHRISTMAS BELL

WANDA L. JONES

The weather was clear and cold as nine-year-old Melody left the Christmas bazaar with her single purchase—a tiny Christmas bell.

"It's a magic Christmas bell," the woman had said.

Melody did not believe in magic any more than she believed in Santa Claus or the tooth fairy.

"Every time it rings, they say, it brings a Christmas blessing, if the owner has the magic of Christmas."

"How do I know if I have this magic?" Melody had questioned. "Maybe the bell wouldn't work for me."

"It would be worth finding out, wouldn't it? After all, what greater good is there than to give blessings to others?"

Even if it was just a plain Christmas bell with no magic at all, it was pretty and had a pure, sweet tone. It looked quite festive pinned now to her coat. As she jumped a snow drift, the bell gave a merry tinkle.

"Well, hello, little Christmas spirit. You sound like Christmas itself coming down the street." Mr. Swenson, the baker, was shoveling snow from the front of his shop.

"Reminds me of a little bell that used to hang on our Christmas tree when my daughter was a little girl. Whenever a draft would tremble the branches, the little bell would tinkle, and my daughter would call out from her bed, 'Is it Santa Claus, Papa?'" The old man's face clouded. "That was a very long time ago. My daughter and her family live far away now. I will not see them this Christmas. But, here now. Won't you come inside the shop? I baked some Christmas cookies this morning."

Melody followed reluctantly, fearing that even a few minutes with this sad old man would only spoil the afternoon.

"They're almond cookies, my daughter's favorite," he went on as he put a plateful on the counter. "I don't know what I was thinking. Six dozen Christmas cookies on Christmas Eve, and the shop closed tomorrow!"

In the warm, steamy bakery the two ate cookies, talked about Christmases past, and to Melody's surprise were soon laughing merrily. Mr. Swenson's eyes grew bright, and Melody knew he was no longer sad.

As she rose to go, Mr. Swenson put several more cookies into a bag. His wrinkled face broke into a smile.

"Such a blessing you have brought me today! I was feeling sad, but I shouldn't have. I have so many happy things to think about. Perhaps I'll even decorate a Christmas tree tonight—with a little bell on it!" he added.

In spite of the cold, a warm feeling inside her persisted all the way down the block. Melody gave a little skip that set her Christmas bell to tinkling.

Suddenly she heard sobs. A little boy was sitting in the snow, his sled overturned. Melody bent over to help him up. The Christmas bell jingled merrily. The tear-streaked face looked up, and the red, swollen eyes fixed themselves on the bell.

Melody jingled the bell again with her finger. "Do you like my bell?" she asked, smiling. "It's a magic bell, you know."

The little boy's eyes grew round with wonder.

"Is it really magic?" he asked shyly.

"For sure," Melody said, taking his hand. "Come on. I'll walk you home."

Four houses down, she left the little boy at his door.

"What kind of magic does it do?" he asked, still awed by the bell.

"It makes things disappear," she replied.

"Like what, for instance?"

"Well, your tears, for one thing. They're all gone."

The boy laughed, squeezed her hand, and disappeared inside.

"Well, little bell, if you don't work wonders! Even if it isn't real magic," Melody said aloud as she headed homeward again.

On the corner a man was standing motionless. Melody knew by the red-tipped cane he held that he was blind. As she made a turn to go around him, her little Christmas bell tinkled sweetly.

"Who's there?" he called out, tilting his head to one side.

"Only me," Melody answered timidly.

"Come here, please," he pleaded. "I've been standing here for quite a long time waiting for someone to help me. You see, I've dropped something in the snow, and I fear I may have covered it up looking for it. Would you take a look? It is a brooch for my wife. I must find it."

Melody knelt and began to brush away the snow. She soon found the brooch and placed it in the grateful man's hands.

"How can I thank you? You have saved me from an unhappy Christmas. It was a blessing you came along when you did."

Another Christmas blessing! thought Melody. She waited for the walk light and bounded across the intersection toward St. Luke's Church. Father Jackson stood on the steps.

"Father Jackson, could I ask you something?" Melody began.

"Of course, Melody," the priest answered. "What is it?"

"Just one question, Father. Is there... could there be magic in a Christmas bell?"

"Magic in a bell?" The priest looked puzzled.

Briefly she told him the woman's claim about the bell. "And it's happened three times on the way home," she said. "Three times it rang and three times someone got a blessing. The woman said it would happen if I had the magic of Christmas. Do I have it, Father Jackson?"

The priest's face softened. "You do, indeed, Melody. You gave three blessings, sure as the world."

"Then it's true? The bell is magic?"

"No, not the bell, little one. The 'magic,' is in you. It's love. That's the magic of Christmas. When you give love to those you meet, you give blessings indeed."

Melody turned toward home, her steps picking up speed. She wanted to think about what Father Jackson had said, but not now. She was too excited, and she felt unusually happy.

She did not notice that the priest was still looking after her or that the tension of a too-busy Christmas was gone from his face. Neither did she hear his words that were swept away by the wind.

"Keep working that magic, little one, and you will discover the real blessing it brings—the happiness that comes to the heart of the one who gives love."

Renewal&Rebirth

As the purse is emptied, the heart is filled.
–VICTOR HUGO

AT CHRISTMAS TOWN

SAM MCGARRITY

*H*ave you ever spent Christmas in a place that linked you so closely to the season that you actually felt at peace with the Christmas spirit? Let me explain. I'm one of those single people who never quite fit anywhere during the holidays. For me, it's the season to feel awkward, and as jolly as I may appear outwardly, inwardly I'm relieved when Christmas is over. Last year I'd planned to sleep through Christmas Day, just as I did the Christmas before.

My editor ruined that plan.

Christmas was almost upon me, when one afternoon he said, "Sam, we want you and The Pup to drive down to McAdenville, North Carolina, during Christmas week. It's a small town just outside of Charlotte. The mill, it seems, has a chaplain, and he's been in touch with us about some sort of light extravaganza there. He claims that McAdenville becomes Christmas Town in December. It's supposed to be famous. See what it's all about, would you?"

As I steered my 1978 Volkswagen van—which still had no heater—south toward McAdenville, I grumbled to The Pup, the Eskimo spitz who travels with me, "Most towns have lights at Christmas, don't they? Why would this one be any different? Famous, he said! It's so obscure it's not even in the road atlas."

I doubted I'd find much there. It would be damp and miserable. I grew up in the South, where it never snows at Christmas—just rains. And the wet cold seeps through and chills you to the bone. Gray skies threatening rain welcomed me to the Southland.

In Gaston County, North Carolina, I turned off Interstate 95 and left behind the rush of traffic speeding to keep pace with the holiday frenzy. I'd arrived.

Coasting down Main Street, which wound like a skein of yarn past neat yards and well-kept homes that proclaimed the past, I noticed that each had been tastefully decorated with traditional greenery, poinsettias, wreaths, and bows. Porch swings and rockers silently waited for warmer days and company to come "sit a spell." They reminded me of the Sundays when our family used to sit and rock on my great-uncle's porch in Georgia.

In the heart of town, where Main Street forked, two blocks of shops offered dining out, gifts, banking, and barbering. Three brick buildings, the original mills built in 1881 by Rufus Y. McAden and around which the town had developed, now housed the headquarters of Stowe-Pharr Mills, a family-owned textile business with plants in four states and the Netherlands. Stowe-Pharr had grown from a two-hundred-man operation, salvaged after the Depression from McAdenville's closed mills and dying town, to an international business employing about 5,000 people. It was the owner and employer of McAdenville.

I walked The Pup along the nearby south fork of the Catawba River, then met with Billy Miller, the chaplain of Stowe-Pharr, who, I hoped, would tell me why this sleepy little town of 960 people, four churches, and one filling station was a Christmas landmark. Instead, standing tall like a steeple and seeming about as serene, he asked with a twinkle in his eye, "Want to come along on a Santa Mission tomorrow morning?"

I'd never heard of such a thing. "How early?" I asked.

"Eight o'clock."

That sounded pretty early to me. I thought Santa conducted his missions at night, but I said, "Okay, I'll go."

In the meantime, it was almost 5:00 P.M. when Billy Miller and I left his office to tour the town. "The lights will be coming on," he announced.

Click, click, click. Suddenly McAdenville glowed in the dusk as I watched a spectacle of 340,000 red, white, and green lights turn on. Circling through the town's magnolias, its pines and cedars and dogwoods, the fantasy of lights stretched up and down Main Street, from yard to yard, around the community center, the churches, around the mill buildings and the lake.

And as night approached, so did the people—in cars from Virginia, Georgia, South Carolina, Tennessee, and the "Ta' Heel State." Bumper-to-bumper, like a graceful red ribbon, they followed the glistening trees and decorated doors through McAdenville. It would have sent tingles through the Grinch (the one who stole Christmas, remember?).

Walking along the streets of Christmas Town with The Pup prancing beside me, I listened and hummed along with the chrono-chimes that pealed carols into the air. They spoke to us, "Fall on your knees. Oh, hear the angel voices."

A sense of joy slowly stole inside me. It didn't matter that I was alone. I wasn't really. There were all of these people waving to me from cars and the sidewalk, wishing me "Merry Christmas!" Children stopped me on the street and asked to pet The Pup. "He's so-o-o soft. Purty dawg," they crooned.

We drifted along, listening to the exclamations of "Well, I declare!" over the lights and the manger scene. We watched a pretend snowman being lovingly hugged by a real little boy. I sang "Jingle Bells" with a couple of kids from out of town just because it seemed appropriate on such a magical night, and I felt myself actually beginning to look forward to the Santa Mission.

The next morning, I joined the Santa Mission in the research lab of Stowe-Pharr. Lab workers had forgone an office party in order to supply some cheer to a young family whose baby had been in and out of the hospital. Nine of us, lugging shopping bags of gifts and boxes of clothes, followed at the heels of Billy Miller, who knew the troubles of everyone in town and led us to the home of this particular family in need. A doll hung from the opening of one large sack; a shovel poked from another. One lady carried a tricycle. My arms were aching! Billy Miller hadn't mentioned that this mission would require muscles.

At a back door, we heard a young woman scolding and hurrying a protesting little boy into the front room. We waited silently. Then she appeared and welcomed us in. "Oh," she faltered, "how can I ever thank you! You don't know how much this means..."

I knew. We were all silent, trying to blink the tears from our eyes, trying to swallow the lumps in our throats. We all remembered hard times and the generosity of friends easing us through holidays of hopelessness. I remembered the down coat friends gave me one Christmas when I couldn't afford a heavy coat. "We're tired of seeing you wear all those sweaters, Sam," they told me as I peeled off the Christmas wrap. That was eight years ago, when I lived with those friends because I couldn't afford a home either.

Silently we each hugged this young mother of three children. I wanted to tell her that life would get better, but I felt embarrassed. I hoped an embrace would express what I couldn't say. And then we bowed our heads for Billy Miller's Christmas blessing over that staggering kitchen table. Before we filed out, he handed her an envelope containing $209, another gift from the research department. So *that* was a Santa Mission.

As I visited in the mills and talked with spinning overhaulers and pin operators, oilers and crillers, inspectors and packers and supervisors and plant managers, I heard of other Santa Missions. The Stowe-Pharr carpenters had collected $1,700 for a colleague in need. Someone in Plant No. 46 had dressed up in a Santa suit and collected donations for a sick child. The McAdenville Women's Club had provided Christmas for another child. Two sisters had decorated a plant wall with a Christmas scene, "just to help people get in the holiday mood."

At holiday gatherings throughout the mills, workers exchanged gifts over homemade casseroles and desserts. They swapped memories of Christmases past. And as one young man in a buffet line whispered to me, "People seem to care about each other here," I began to understand that Christmas Town was more than just lights and decorations.

I should mention, though, that the lights too were a symbol of caring that began with Mr. William J. Pharr, the company leader from 1939 to 1981. "He was a man who loved people," I was told over and over. "He would go up to workers and hug them and tell them how much they meant to him. It didn't matter how much oil or grease or lint they were wearing that day. That's the kind of man he was." Under the careful direction of his wife, Catherine Stowe Pharr, and with the help of a team of men, the lighting of McAdenville's trees became a thirty-three-year tradition that grew from nine trees to 348. And each year, Stowe-Pharr pays the electric bill.

In 1950, Mr. Pharr brought the Yule Log Celebration to McAdenville. And along with parents, children, and a brass band, I joined in the fun of following the thirty-ninth log dragged up Main Street.

It was a rainy, misty night—the kind that would ordinarily have chilled me to the bone. But I felt surrounded by warm people whose compassion for one another was ushering in the spirit of the Christ Child. These were people who were used to being told they were loved by the company's chief executive officer. I know, because I read those words by him in the company newspaper. These were people who were comfortable praying together. I know, because I bowed my head with them that night in front of the burning Yule log as Catherine Ann Carstarphen, the chief executive officer's wife, led us in prayer. These were people who faced their joys and sorrows with a chaplain who advised them and knelt with them and joked with them.

This was a different world from the big city I had just left, a city where escaping Christmas would have been easy. Here there was no escaping it. Nor did I want to. I already felt a part of it, and I wanted to share it with people I loved.

And so, on Christmas Eve, I decided to continue on in the spirit of the season. "We're going down to Georgia," I told The Pup, "to visit Grandmother, and my aunt and cousins." We didn't have gifts, but maybe just a caring spirit would be gift enough. I'd rediscovered it there in Christmas Town, and I was going to be sure to take it with me on the road.

Sometimes our fate resembles a fruit tree in winter. Who would think that these branches would turn green again and bloom, but we hope it, we know it.

−JOHANN W. GOETHE

COMING HOME

AMY HAUSER

A murky drizzle saturated Duluth's West Michigan Street, darkening the sidewalk that my husband, Nolan, carefully moved along, counting each pace, each solitary division in the pavement, his hands jammed deep in his jean pockets. He paused in front of an empty lot choked with litter and weeds. Then he pointed to it and turned slowly toward the car, where I sat inside peering through a ragged porthole I'd rubbed in the window-fog with the palm of my hand. The rain slanted down on his back, and his glasses were streaked. "This was it," he called, nodding for emphasis.

"Right here."

Nolan had found it, the spot where the Blomstrom house had stood. We'd traveled here to Minnesota from our Pennsylvania home, following the thread of Nolan's restless search for his past. I couldn't help thinking what courage he had. My husband is a strong, loving man, but quiet and private. Rarely does he speak of the day in 1960 when his ten-year-old world came apart.

Through the years, though, I've pieced together the story.

Nolan had run all the way home from the park that blistering July afternoon to his house on West Michigan. Stunned onlookers stood in the Blom-strom's neat yard. Neighbors craned out of their windows. Angling his way breathlessly through to the front of the crowd, Nolan suddenly froze. There on the grass lay his mother, cradled by his older brother Ronnie. Then a family friend was leading Nolan away and trying to explain the terrible truth that would change his life and the lives of his seven brothers and sisters forever: Nolan's mother and father had been the victims of a tragic accident.

As Nolan now stared through the downpour at the forlorn tangle of undergrowth that was once his boyhood home, I imagined the ghosts sweeping through his memory: policemen milling around the house, reporters scribbling furiously and photographers snapping away, the hysterical wail of the ambulance rushing away his dying parents as a neighbor blotted Nolan's tears with her apron and held him back.

I wished I could wipe it all away for him, all that sorrow and pain in his past, push it all out with love. Though I knew this was his own private moment, I couldn't help going over and putting my arm around him, my fin-gertips barely reaching his far shoulder. He leaned slightly into my embrace.

After the deaths of their parents, the Blomstrom kids were scattered. Initially two went with relatives; Nolan and five others were taken in by a local minister and his wife, the Hausers. Family pets were given away, possessions sold off, the house closed up. Eventually the Hausers moved to South Dakota, then Minnesota, where they finalized adoption of the four youngest children. Time passed. The kids grew up and moved on, separated by time and distance. Never again would they celebrate Christmases or birthdays together as a family. They had faded apart forever, it seemed, under the shadow of tragedy.

Yet something, some inexplicable thread, still bound the children together.

Through the decades and across geography they managed not to lose touch completely. A graduation announcement, or word of a wedding or birth, got passed around in the course of a year or so. News circled: an unexpected phone call, an impromptu postcard. One sister married her high school sweetheart; the youngest girl married a minister. Nolan and I were teachers. We married in 1977 and lived in Marion, Indiana. The one mystery was Ronnie. He dropped out of sight sometime in the '70s, not to be heard from since.

We turned and headed to the car, and Nolan took just one quick last glance back over his shoulder before we climbed in and he started the engine for the trip home. The wipers began to slap the raindrops off the windshield as we eased down West Michigan. For the first time in our marriage, I felt truly connected to Nolan's past. *It must be so hard for him*, I thought as I studied his coppery profile, as handsome to me as ever, his eyes soft and blue. *Thank God for the children, for the school.*

Our coming to the Milton Hershey School in the rolling countryside of Hershey, Pennsylvania, is, we believe, intrinsically tied up with what happened to the Blomstrom family that fateful summer day in Nolan's childhood.

In the early '80s, schools began to close in the Midwest. I'd left teaching to stay home with our two kids, Nathan and Sarah. With layoffs imminent, Nolan's search for another position proved futile. Our daily prayers for someone to buy our house seemed to no avail. We needed to sell in order to move to more fertile job hunting grounds. "Lord," I pleaded, "what do You want us to do?"

Late one night back in western Pennsylvania in the small country house where I grew up, my mother lay awake in bed. She was anxious about our job situation. She'd prayed and prayed about it. Now she got up out of bed and paced. Suddenly she sat down and wrote a letter to an unusual school she heard of in Hershey, asking about jobs for us. It was not the type of school that would normally have appealed to us. Yet Mom had felt compelled somehow in the middle of the night to get out of bed and write that letter. When she received the applications, she passed them on to us with a sheepish apology: "Being houseparents at a boarding school probably wasn't what you had in mind, but I was at my wit's end for a way to help you."

Houseparents? We read the brochures and applications. *That doesn't sound like us. We're teachers.*

We were in no position to be choosy. We still hadn't had a nibble on the house when we decided to drive the 600 miles to Hershey for an interview.

But a wonderful, mysterious thing began happening in those green farming hills of Pennsylvania. Even before we got to Hershey, a feeling overtook us, a growing feeling of calm, a kind of peace we'd been praying for. We hardly spoke the last few miles.

We listened intently during our interview with the residential director of the school, who explained its history to us. When Milton S. Hershey, the chocolate magnate, died in 1945, the beneficiary of his fortune was the school he had established, originally for orphaned boys. Spread today across a 9,000-acre campus, eighty-nine student homes accommodate 1,100 boys and girls. "Everything is provided at no cost to their parents," he said. "They're here because in some way their lives have been disrupted. Maybe it's been the death of a parent, or a difficult divorce. Some parents just want their kids away from a bad environment at home. All are here for a solid education. They live in homes with special couples we call houseparents, who provide a stable, nurturing environment where the students can grow and succeed."

It was a moment, one of those clear and vibrant moments, when you know your life is changing. Nolan's eyes met mine and we understood *right then* that we would come here to live with these children. No hesitation, no second thoughts. That calm sense that we'd been led to Hershey was stronger than ever. Yes, Nolan knew these kids. He'd been one of them.

We drove back to Marion. And like a blessing, the house we couldn't sell had a buyer the day we returned. It was just a matter of packing now.

Today we live at Student Home Stiegel with our children and 11 boys, aged ten to fourteen. Our lives have become interlocked with those of our students and the school. We've seen many lives change—but none more amazingly than our own.

One by one Nolan's siblings visited. Hershey became a common ground for the scattered family, a magnet, a place they came back to. The filament that had mysteriously connected them through the years irresistibly pulled them together once more, this time permanently.

First it was Nolan's youngest brother, Terry, and his wife who moved here from Oklahoma to be houseparents. They now live across the hill at Student Home Moldavia. Then came sister Donna and her husband from Rhode Island. They're not only houseparents, they're also our next-door neighbors. From New Mexico came the eldest brother, Keith, and his wife and daughters. Then it was Neal and his family from Illinois. All of them drawn by this remarkable school, all of them houseparents to children whose lives in so many ways parallel their own. Sisters Diane from Mississippi and Kay from South Dakota visited this summer. We joked that we wouldn't be surprised if they too showed up one day to stay.

This Christmas season Nolan, Nathan, Sarah, and I will join together with Nolan's brothers and sisters and their families at one of our homes for a traditional family meal. There amid the holiday scents of fresh pine and burning candles, and the singing of carols about a silent night, we'll witness once again a miracle of our own. Nathan and Sarah will look around at their aunts and uncles and cousins, nineteen of us in all, together again because that is how families are meant to be. Not even the tragedy on West Michigan Street could destroy the loving force that bound this incredible family together through the years.

Only Ronnie is still missing.

More than lights or mistletoe, reindeer or candy canes, Christmas is about home, about family. It is most of all the story of a family—Mary, Joseph, and Jesus, a family that grew to include all of us.

We'll sit down to Christmas dinner again this year thankful for the slow motion miracle that drew this family close again; and in our hearts we'll remember Ronnie, wherever he may be, and in our prayers we will bring him home too.

In the time we have it is surely our duty to do all the good we can to all the people we can in all the ways we can.

—WILLIAM BARCLAY

THE MAN WHO WANTED TO GO HOME

JIMMY GUPTON

nother Christmas coming…toy commercials and holiday specials on television. And here I was, an old man spending another evening in front of the tube.

Why, Lord? I asked Him for the thousandth time. *Why won't you just go ahead and take me home?*

I'd been a Christian all my life and figured the Almighty didn't mind my taking a familiar tone with Him. *Ninety-three years is long enough on this earth. I've lived a full life, and I can't see where I'm much good to You or anyone else anymore.*

When my wife was alive it was different. But Bess had been gone now seven years, and lately it was getting harder to go through the motions. Christmas, for example. I hadn't even bothered to get the big silver tree out of the box in the attic this year. It was a pretty thing, but attaching 150 branches was a big job. After my eyes went bad I'd had to take an ice pick to feel for the holes. With only me here, why bother?

A rock group came on the screen to sing "Jingle Bells." *You see, Lord, I'm not going to be able to take care of this place much longer, and You know I don't want to go somewhere else.* My two sons and their families kept asking me to move in with one of them, but I'm a stubborn kind of fellow. I liked it here, liked my independence.

This past year, though... It was a small house, but it was getting to be too much. The roof was leaking, the wallpaper peeling. *Why can't I just come home, Lord, and not fool with an interim move?*

On the screen now were pictures of the Salvation Army shelter in downtown Charlotte, part of a series on homelessness at Christmas. "There are over two hundred women sleeping here tonight," an announcer said, "out of work and out of hope." I sure felt sorry for those people, but I hardly had enough money to cover my own expenses, much less make a donation. At about ten o'clock I switched off the set, turned off the lights, and said my usual prayers before climbing into bed.

Instead of falling asleep, though, I kept seeing those women at the shelter. I'd always given to the poor when I was able. Surely it was someone else's turn now. But that news report wouldn't let me alone. There were those women needing help. Just like me, I thought.

I sat up in bed. What if two needy folks were to put their needs together? What if one of these women were to move in here, take care of the house in exchange for a place to live?

The next morning I telephoned the shelter. "If you're serious, Mr. Gupton," the manager said, "I'll ask around."

A few days after Christmas he called back: "Would you consider taking in a married couple?"

"Well, now..." I hadn't counted on *two* people. "It's such a small house," I apologized. "The spare room's barely big enough for one."

"What I was thinking," the man went on, "was that the wife could keep house and the husband could look after the yard. As for the size of the room, I'm sure anything with a door on it would look like a palace to them right now."

The manager paused a moment to let this sink in. "I think I've got the perfect couple. Tony and Pam Davis."

Both Davises had lost their jobs. Unable to meet rent payments, they'd been evicted from their home, and ended up sleeping at the shelter at night and job hunting during the day. "It's hard to impress an employer, wearing wrinkled clothing, having no permanent address."

"Send them on over," I said. "We'll give it a try."

It looked as though it was going to work. Pam was a little shy at first, but before the week was out we were chatting like old friends. She told me she'd been a waitress while Tony worked as a carpet installer, until both places of employment went out of business the same month. With downcast eyes she described what it had been like to be in a Salvation Army shelter at Christmastime.

It was nice to have someone keeping house, cooking meals, taking care of the yard again. Wonderful to have them care enough to escort me to the senior citizens' center, to drive me to church.

About three months after they'd come, though, Pam said she needed to talk to me. The two of us had just finished lunch; Tony had found a job with another carpet installation company and was gone during the day.

"I don't know how to say this, Mr. Gupton," she began.

Oh, no! I thought. *She's going to tell me they're moving out now that Tony's working.*

Pam got up and started piling dishes in the sink. "I know I should have told you in the beginning," she said, "but I was afraid you wouldn't let us stay—and you might want us to leave after you hear this. But I can't put off telling you any longer. . . "

She twisted the dishrag in her hands. "You see, I. . . I'm. . . " She lifted her dark eyes to stare into mine. "I'm going to have a baby."

So that was it! "Well, you're right about one thing," I said. "I hadn't counted on three of you, that's for sure." She turned away, looking down at the sink. "But I certainly can't let you go back on the streets," I assured her. "Not with a baby coming." I tried to keep my voice calm, but my mind was shouting, A baby! Where will we put a baby?

"I know there's not much room here," Pam said, as if reading my thoughts. "But if we move the dresser out of our room, I'm sure we could squeeze a small crib in, and I'll try to keep the baby quiet so it won't disturb you too much."

The months flew by. Pam shifted the tiny room around to sandwich a crib between the bed and the wall, bought diapers and bottles, and began a whirlwind of painting and wallpapering all over the house.

And before I knew it, a redheaded baby girl named Sabrina arrived. Pam tried to keep her quiet and out of my way as much as possible. Soon she was three months old, then five months old, and then it was the middle of December and almost Christmas again.

I was sitting in the living room one evening reading the second chapter of Luke as I always did at this time of year. "And she brought forth her firstborn Son," I read, "and laid Him in a manger, because there was no room for them in the inn." (verse 7).

That must have saddened God, I thought, feeling pretty good that I'd found room for the Davis family, though in some ways it had been an inconvenience. Even as I thought about the crowded inn, though, I knew that wasn't the point of the story. What God had wanted, far more than a room at the inn, was for people to open their hearts and make room for His Son.

Perhaps that's what He'd been trying to get me to do. Sure, I'd made room for the Davises in my house, but maybe God had been trying to get me to make room in my heart.

The winter wind was beating at the old windows, seeping round the newspapers Pam had stuffed into the cracks. I got up and stoked the fire in the wood stove, had to keep the place warm for the baby. *You know*, I told myself, *if we slid the couch back against the wall, I believe there'd be room for a playpen in here. Can't keep a growing child cooped up in a bedroom.*

I walked over to the stairs. "Tony! Pam!" I called.

"What is it, Mr. Gupton?" Tony asked, hurrying down.

"Is something wrong?" said Pam, following behind him, alarm in her eyes.

"You bet something's wrong," I said. "Here it is, almost Christmas, and we don't have a tree up!"

"We thought about that," Tony admitted, "but trees are so expensive."

"That's so," I agreed. "'But I happen to know where there's a beautiful tree just waiting to be put up. It's in a box in the attic now, but when it's standing tall and grand with the colored lights beaming across its silver branches, you never saw anything so pretty in all your life. With a child in the house, we've got to have a Christmas tree!"

Tony and Pam raced up the rickety stairs to the attic and dragged down the bulky box. Pam unpacked the branches; I fluffed out the tinsel "needles" and passed them to Tony to insert in the holes. It was fun doing it together. I coached Tony as he set the tree in the revolving stand I'd made out of an old TV antenna many years before. Then I switched on the multicolored floodlight and sat back to enjoy their ooh's and aah's as the tree started to turn like a silver ballerina.

About that time, we heard a hungry wail from upstairs. Pam ran up and brought Sabrina down. Pam looked surprised, but pleased, when I motioned for her to hand the baby to me while she went off to the kitchen to heat a bottle. We sat there, eyeing each other silently. I felt kind of awkward. After all, it had been some time since I'd conversed with a young child.

Sabrina studied my face intently, and for a moment I thought she was going to cry. But instead she broke into a laugh and reached a chubby little hand toward my cheek. I laughed too when I realized she was trying to catch the fleeting reflections from the tree. The touch of her hand made me think of another Child, born on Christmas so many years ago.

I looked at Tony, arranging candles in the window, and listened to Pam, humming a carol out in the kitchen. And I whispered a prayer to the One who has our times in His keeping.

Thank You, Lord, for letting me see another Christmas . . . for leaving me here though I fussed and fretted. Sometimes it takes a baby to remind an old man what Your world is all about.

*Consider how much more you often suffer from
your anger and grief than from those very things
for which you are angry and grieved.*
—MARCUS AURELIUS

SHINING THROUGH

SHARI SMYTH

In our nightly dinner table reading of the Advent calendar, the Wise Men were almost to Bethlehem. It was fifteen-year-old Sanna's turn to read aloud, and she was flying through it as if she couldn't get them to the manger fast enough. I gritted my teeth as her younger brother, Jonathan, stared at her comically, his victory complete when Sanna lost her concentration and dissolved into giggles. Laura, our seventeen-year-old, seemed to be above it all, chewing quietly.

It's not the same anymore, I brooded, trying to cap my disappointment. *Our house used to be full of Christmas spirit.* But the kids weren't as wrapped up anymore in the old traditions they once cherished, like reading the Advent calendar every night.

After dinner I returned the calendar to the refrigerator door and loaded the dishwasher, daydreaming about the annual Christmas pageant the kids used to put on for Whitney and me. I'd let them raid the linen closet for costumes. One year our scruffy black dog was the third Wise Man. Her tail drooped in embarrassment through her bed-sheet getup. Now I glanced at her as she waddled, old and stiff, across the kitchen to her bowl, and I wondered if she remembered too.

Things picked up a little the next day when our oldest, Wendy, returned from college. "It's me!" her voice erupted as she banged through the kitchen door, gorged luggage skidding across the linoleum. I call Wendy my whirlwind child. I was forever telling her to slow down and *think*—generally to no avail. But Whitney and I were grateful for her impulsive generosity when she treated her brother and sisters to dinner out that night. It gave us time to apply the final holiday touches at home. The house was spotless and smelled of lemon and pine and fresh-baked pies. I wanted to give my best for the coming of the Christ Child. When Whitney finally flicked on the tree lights, I felt the stirrings of the old Christmas spirit. "There," I sighed, leaning against him. "Perfect."

The next night was Christmas Eve. The house buzzed with all of us getting dressed for church. Whitney, Jonathan, and I were going to the five o'clock service. My daughters preferred the later one. Between, we'd meet at a restaurant for dinner. "See you at seven, girls," Whitney called as we left. Just before I tugged the front door shut I turned for a last look at our handiwork. *Yes, it really is beginning to feel like Christmas.*

The five o'clock service was boisterous. Nervous mothers helped small children into costumes. I felt a stab of envy, remembering when I helped ready my little ones for the pageant. I felt tired from all the hard work the holidays demand. The lights dimmed and the little stage became a stable. The simplicity of it reminded me of how stark that first Christmas had actually been, how transient. The scene closed with an enormous glitter-covered star leading the Wise Men to the manger, where they knelt with their gifts. We all sang "We Three Kings of Orient Are," and it was over.

Whitney pulled into the restaurant parking lot and my eyes quickly scanned the cars for Wendy's beatup old Dodge. We went inside. Rotund candles burned in pine wreaths on the tables. Christmas music spilled from concealed speakers. Where *were* my girls?

The waiter seated us at a window table. I was grateful to have a view of the lot so that I could stop worrying the minute the old Dodge made an appearance. When it finally did, irritation and relief battled for control of my feelings. Then I saw the girls' glum faces as they filed by the window and came inside.

They took their seats silently. I wasn't sure I wanted to hear the explanation I knew was coming. "Mom," Wendy began, knotting a green napkin that proclaimed MERRY CHRISTMAS, "there's been a fire, just a tiny fire in the kitchen, but it made a lot of soot."

The menu fell out of my hands. "How much *soot*?"

Then Wendy was crying, huge rolling tears I hadn't seen her shed in years. She'd been melting some wax to do her legs (a continental alternative to shaving she'd picked up in France), and in her typical haste she thought she'd turned off the burner but in fact hadn't. That's how the pan caught fire. "At least the house didn't burn up," Laura offered, looking for that silver lining in a very dark cloud. "Thank God you guys are all safe," said Whitney.

"I'm really sorry, Mom," Wendy gulped.

The minute we walked in the house the choking stench of soot hit me. The downstairs was a disaster—ceilings, walls, furniture, Christmas decorations, the Nativity set—all overlaid with a grimy black film. I swung open the cupboards and slammed them shut. The soot had got in there too, on our dishes and silverware, our spice tins and canned goods. My pies were ruined. The soles of our shoes turned black from the floor. My hands were black.

On the refrigerator the Advent calendar with the picture of the Wise Men was black. . . the star too, as if it had burned out. And for me it had. We retreated upstairs and spent the night in the house. But the smell of smoke was so bad, and the kitchen virtually unusable, that the next morning we had to abandon our home. Christmas morning.

The only place we could find to have dinner was a hotel coffee shop. We just didn't feel up to horning in on friends. "This is kind of like no room at the inn," Whitney commented as we ate hamburgers.

"Yeah," Laura agreed eagerly, "I guess things fell apart in Bethlehem too." My husband grinned and my children laughed—and I tried, I really tried, to join in. But the anger wouldn't leave me. Wendy had apologized. She felt terrible and had learned a lesson, she informed me. I'd said I forgave her. The insurance company would pay for everything, even our hotel bill, until the downstairs could be cleaned and painted. Yet in my heart I struggled with resentment that seemed to grow larger every time I thought about our ruined Christmas. Ruined.

The next day we were all going to go bowling together. I just couldn't. "You go," I told Whitney. "I need some time." Wendy gave me a squeeze as they filed out the door.

After they'd gone I threw on a coat and headed for the house, thinking that I'd take down some of the decorations and clean them off as best I could. I needed to do something.

Fog and drizzle hid the house till I was in the drive. Inside, the air still reeked of smoke. If anything, even more of the wretched soot had settled. The place was stale and depressing. I'd made a mistake in coming.

I began taking the decorations off the tree, wiping them delicately with a rag. Soon my hands were pitch black, my nose was clogged. Was this really the same perfect room where I'd stood with Whitney and felt the coming of Christmas?

The ornament slid from my fingertips as tears filled my eyes and carved rivulets down my sooty cheeks. I'd had a feeling about this Christmas. Even before the fire. The kids seemed different—older, jaded. No one cared much about all the lovely holiday trappings I held so dear. I pulled myself to a chair and collapsed.

Then my eyes landed on the crèche. Instinctively I reached out with one hand while trying to smear away my messy tears with the other. I plucked the baby Jesus from His crib. He lay in the palm of my hand, gray with soot, ruined, just like everything else in the room, like everything else this Christmas. I wiped the figurine on my old denim shirtsleeve. My teardrops helped clear away some of the dirt. I wiped a little more. And more. I wanted at least this one thing to be clean, to be perfect. Soon the Christ Child shone.

And then I began to feel it, finally, for the first time that year, the spirit of Christmas. *Amazing*, I thought, *how this little figure, wiped clean, shines through it all.*

There were no decorations when He came down from heaven that first Christmas. The world was a mess, wildly imperfect, just as it is today. But that didn't prevent God's love for us from bursting through in Bethlehem.

Christmases are never the same. They change from year to year, and they are never really perfect, no matter how hard we try to force them to be so. What is perfect is the miracle in Bethlehem 2,000 years ago and the love of God that continues to burst through the chaos of human imperfection; Christmas is finding the Christ Child radiant beneath the daily grime of life.

With a prayer of thanks I carefully replaced the Infant in the manger. The rest of the cleanup could wait. I had to find Whitney and the kids. I knew they'd probably be eating hamburgers at the hotel coffee shop. I couldn't wait to join them.

If angels come not to minister unto us, it is because we do not invite them, it is because we keep the door closed through which they might otherwise enter.
—RALPH W. TRINE

STORM ON THE MOUNTAIN

SHIRLEY BRAVERMAN

Through the swirling snowfall in the San Jacinto Mountains, I could see Ray the forest ranger on the road in front of me. I was so angry and in such a hurry to get to my cabin, I was tempted to ignore him when he flagged me down.

I pumped the brake and brought my truck, Betsy, to a stop. "Look, Ray," I said through clenched teeth, "please don't tell me I can't go through. I only live a mile-and-a-half up the mountain, and I'm not exactly inexperienced at driving in the snow."

He frowned and I could see his nose was almost frozen. "I don't have any authority to turn back residents," he said, "but it's been coming down hard for three hours now. You can hardly see. And there could be an avalanche anytime."

"I'll drive slow," I promised, and went on my way.

I'd driven home in torrential rain, pounding hail, icy sleet, and when the clouds crept up the mountain and sat down on the road like they owned it. But I had to admit this blinding snowstorm was some of the worst weather I'd seen. I hunched over the wheel, focusing on the road. Not that the road got all my attention. I was hot with anger at my daughter-in-law.

My husband, daughter, and son had been killed in an accident on a Los Angeles freeway less than three years before, and not a day had gone by when I didn't struggle through all the feelings that still tormented me in the aftermath of that tragedy. My cabin in the San Jacinto Mountains was my only refuge from the harsh realities of life. My son's wife, crazy with grief, had taken up with a brute of a man. I'd told her he was no good. I told her he wasn't right for the kids. I told her to leave him. But she'd ignored me. Then he became abusive. She'd finally left him; and now, after all this time, she wanted my help. Wanted to move in with me so she could go back to school. With me, in my tiny mountain cabin! We'd had a terrible fight back at her apartment in the city. The kids had cried and I'd stormed out.

I squinted into the whirling snow. *I need my peace and quiet. I deserve it*, I thought. But I knew the real reason I didn't want to help. I no longer had the heart; whatever love I'd had to give had died with my family.

It was getting harder to see out the windshield. This was exactly why Ray didn't want to let me up here. But I was stubborn, set in my ways. I knew it. When my daughter-in-law had called me stubborn, however, I accused her of being insensitive.

I banged the flat of my hand on the steering wheel. I couldn't see a darn thing. Nothing but darkness ahead. Like my future.

If only things could be different, I thought. *If only I could start over again without all this anger and hurt in my soul.* I held the wheel tight with both hands, peering into the darkness.

Then, in the midst of it, a sunlit patch opened up before me. A column of snow seemed to dance in front of my car. I gasped and hit the brake. There in the center of the column was the image of an old woman. She looked like my dear grandmother who'd nurtured me as a child. Who'd cared for me when my parents went to work in a factory during World War II. Who'd saved her money all year to buy me a wonderful Christmas dress. The vision held out a hand as if in warning.

"Go back!" she said. "Go back!"

Had I really heard the words through the moaning of the storm, or were they just in my head? I blinked and looked again. The sunlight was still there, but the image of the woman was gone.

I could feel the tears streaming down my face, the beating of my heart within my breast. I felt as I had as a child, surrounded and nourished by my grandmother's love. Love I had thought I would never feel again. Love I should be passing on...

To my left was the only turnout on the road. I threw my truck into gear, turned around, and headed down the mountain the way I'd come.

When I got back to the ranger station, Ray ran out to meet me. "Thank God you're okay!" he yelled. "An avalanche hit minutes after you left. The spotters called it in on the radio. It took out the road above the turnout."

"You're welcome to spend the night with my wife and me," Ray offered. "Might be a few days before the road is cleared."

"That's very kind of you," I said awkwardly, "but I've got to go down to the city again. My grandkids and their mother need me." He waved me on.

When my grandmother lay ailing at the end of her life, I had been heart-broken at the thought of never seeing her again. She'd promised me that when she got to heaven she would make sure I was always watched over. On a snowy mountain road God had sent an angel I could not fail to recognize to redirect my life. I had a new reason for living: to be the grandmother that my grandmother had been to me, to share the love she had shared with me. I gunned the truck and said, "Come on, Betsy. I have family waiting."

*For everything you have missed, you have gained
something else.*
−RALPH WALDO EMERSON

THE CHRISTMAS NO GIFTS CAME

DRUE DUKE

'll never forget the first Christmas I spent away from my parents and my sisters; the Christmas I thought I'd receive no gifts.

I was a war bride, living in El Paso, Texas, where my soldier husband was stationed. Because we were saving for a trip to California the next month, we agreed we would not exchange Christmas gifts.

We bought a tiny artificial tree and put it on a table, ready to receive the gifts we knew would come from our families in Georgia and Connecticut. Each time the mail truck stopped at the apartment house, I expected the buzzer to our first-floor apartment to sound. But this did not happen.

Christmas Eve came, and around seven o'clock that night Bob was at the hall telephone, calling the post office. As soon as he walked into our apartment, I knew from his face what he had learned. There would be no more deliveries tonight. There would be no gifts to open on Christmas morning.

"I'm sorry, honey," he said. "I'm sure our folks just didn't realize how long it would take for packages to get all the way across the country."

I looked at our pitiful little tree and thought of the floor-to-ceiling tree I knew would be in the music room back home.

"It's not fair!" I cried. "We're way out here, all alone, and we've got no

Christmas!"

Just then our door buzzer sounded. Bob opened the door, and a young man dressed in a khaki uniform like Bob's stood there.

"Merry Christmas!" he said. "I think we must be the only ones left in the building. I saw you in the hall, using the phone." He stuck out his hand. "I'm Ned Rogers from the third floor. My wife and I wondered if you'd come up for some fruitcake and coffee and go to the midnight service with us?"

Bob accepted readily, and I was not opposed to going. After all, what else was there to do?

It was a pleasant enough evening. The four of us exchanged background information about ourselves. They could not go home to Ohio because Ned, like Bob, could not get a furlough over Christmas. They sympathized with us over our lack of gifts, and I moved my chair to keep from seeing their pile of gaily wrapped packages. I was actually seething with anger at our families, at the post office, at everything and everybody; and worse, I was jealous of these people who were trying to be our friends.

I was just about as poor a candidate for church attendance that night as anyone could be. But I climbed with the others into the bus that took us to the downtown Methodist church.

The church was crowded and we had to sit at one side near the back. There was no light except from candles burning in the altar area and in each of the windows along the side walls. The organ played softly, and there was a gentle hum of voices as friends wished each other a Merry Christmas.

Abruptly, the music stopped. A hush fell over the crowd. And then from the nearby town clock came the first vibrating bong-g-g of midnight.

Instantly light flooded the church, as though a million watts of electricity had been fed in. The heavy vestibule doors were flung open, and the glorious announcement, "Joy to the world, the Lord is come!" rang out from a white-robed choir moving down both aisles toward the altar. The congregation swept to its feet and raised its voice to join the choir. Above it all, I could hear the clock still proclaiming the birth of a new day, Christmas Day.

My tight, angry, bitter, jealous heart soared within me until my body could not contain it. It burst into a thousand fragments of remorse and repentance for itself and left in its place a glowing flood of love and gratitude.

"The Lord is come! Let earth receive her King!"

My voice rang out with the others. My eyes sought Bob's face and found him smiling. His hand reached out to find mine. And, as with fingers laced together, we sang lustily, we both knew the truth—we were not without gifts. The material things that come wrapped in fancy paper are only symbolic of the *real* Gift of Christmas, the One wrapped in love and swaddling clothes—the Christ Child, Son of the Living God.

The moment you start moving in the direction of accomplishment, you will find that life will accommodate you.
—JACK ADDINGTON

THE MAN WHO MISSED CHRISTMAS

J. EDGAR PARKS

On Christmas Eve, as usual, George Mason was the last to leave the office. He stood for a moment at the window, watching the hurrying crowds below, the strings of colored Christmas lights, the fat Santa Clauses on the street corners. He was a slender man in his late thirties, this George Mason, not conspicuously successful or brilliant, but a good executive—he ran his office efficiently and well.

Abruptly he turned and walked over to a massive safe set into the far wall. He spun the dials and swung the heavy door open. A light went on, revealing a vault of polished steel as large as a small room. George Mason carefully propped a chair against the open door of the safe and stepped inside.

He took three steps forward, tilting his head so that he could see the square of white cardboard taped just above the topmost row of strong-boxes. On the card a few words were written. George Mason stared at those words, remembering. . . .

Exactly one year ago he had entered this selfsame vault. He had planned a rather expensive, if solitary, evening, had decided he might need a little additional cash. He had not bothered to prop the door; ordinarily friction held the balanced mass of metal in place. But only that morning the people who serviced the safe had cleaned and oiled it. And then, behind George Mason's back, slowly, noiselessly, the ponderous door swung shut. There was a click of springlocks. The automatic light went out, and he was trapped—entombed in the sudden and terrifying dark.

Instantly, panic seized him. He hurled himself at the unyielding door. He gave a hoarse cry; the sound was like an explosion in that confined place. In the silence that followed, he heard the frantic thudding of his heart. Through his mind flashed all the stories he had heard of men found suffocated in timevaults. No timeclock controlled this mechanism; the safe would remain locked until it was opened from the outside. Tomorrow morning.

Then the sickening realization struck him. No one would come tomorrow morning—tomorrow was Christmas Day.

Once more he flung himself at the door, shouting wildly, beating with his hands until he sank on his knees exhausted. Silence again, high-pitched, singing silence that seemed deafening.

George Mason was no smoker; he did not carry matches. Except for the tiny luminous dial of his watch, the darkness was absolute. The blackness almost had texture: it was tangible, stifling. The time now was 6:15. More than thirty-six hours would pass before anyone entered the office. Thirty-six hours in a steel box three feet wide, eight feet long, seven feet high. Would the oxygen last, or would...

Like a flash of lightning a memory came to him, dim with the passage of time. What had they told him when they installed the safe? Something about a safety measure for just such a crisis as this.

Breathing heavily, he felt his way around the floor. The palms of his hands were sweating. But in the far righthand corner, just above the floor, he found it: a small, circular opening some two inches in diameter. He thrust his finger into it and felt, faint but unmistakable, a cool current of air.

The tension release was so sudden that he burst into tears. But at last he sat up. Surely he would not have to stay trapped for the full thirty-six hours. Somebody would miss him, would make inquiries, would come to release him...

But who? He was unmarried and lived alone. The maid who cleaned his apartment was just a servant; he had always treated her as such. He had been invited to spend Christmas Eve with his brother's family, but children got on his nerves and expected presents.

A friend had asked him to go to a home for elderly people on Christmas Day and play the piano—George Mason was a good musician. But he had made some excuse or other; he had intended to sit at home listening to some new recordings he was giving himself for Christmas.

George Mason dug his nails into the palms of his hands until the pain balanced the misery in his mind. He had thrown away his chances. Nobody would come and let him out. Nobody, nobody ...

Marked by the luminous hands of the watch, the leaden-footed seconds ticked away. He slept a little, but not much. He felt no hunger, but he was tormented by thirst. Miserably the whole of Christmas Day went by, and the succeeding night...

On the morning after Christmas, the head clerk came into the office at the usual time. He opened the safe but did not bother to swing the heavy door wide. Then he went on into his private office.

No one saw George Mason stagger out into the corridor, run to the water cooler, and drink great gulps of water. No one paid any attention to him as he descended to the street and took a taxi home.

There he shaved, changed his wrinkled clothes, ate some breakfast, and returned to his office, where his employees greeted him pleasantly but casually.

On his way to lunch that day he met several acquaintances, but not a single one had noticed his Christmas absence. He even met his own brother, who was a member of the same luncheon club, but his brother failed to ask if had enjoyed Christmas.

Grimly, inexorably, the truth closed in on George Mason. He had vanished from human society during the great festival of brotherhood and fellowship, and no one had missed him at all.

Reluctantly, almost with a sense of dread, George Mason began to think about the true meaning of Christmas. Was it possible that he had been blind all these years, blind with selfishness, with indifference, with pride? Wasn't Christmas the time when men went out of their way to share with one another the joy of Christ's birth? Wasn't giving, after all, the essence of Christmas because it marked the time God gave His own Son to the world?

All through the year that followed, with little hesitant deeds of kindness, with small, unnoticed acts of unselfishness, George Mason tried to prepare himself…

Now, once more, it was Christmas Eve.

Slowly he backed out of the safe, closed it. He touched its grim steel face lightly, almost affectionately, as if it were an old friend. He picked up his hat, coat, and certain bundles. Then he left the office and descended to the busy street.

There he goes now in his black overcoat and hat, the same George Mason as a year ago. Or is it? He walks a few blocks, then flags a taxi, anxious not to be late. His nephews are expecting him to help them trim the tree. Afterwards, he is taking his brother and his sister-in-law to a Christmas play. Why is he so inexpressibly happy? Why does this jostling against others, laden as he is with bundles, exhilarate and delight him?

Perhaps the card has something to do with it, the card he taped inside his office safe last New Year's Day. On the card is written, in George Mason's own hand: *To love people, to be indispensable somewhere, that is the purpose of life. That is the secret of happiness.*

There is a reason for everything;
nothing happens without the permission of God.
—ALLAN KARDEC

A LOAD OF COAL

H.N. COOK

On Christmas Eve 1948, the snow was coming down hard, blowing and swirling around my old two-ton dump truck as I drove across the West Virginia mountains. It had been snowing for hours and had accumulated eight to ten inches deep. My job at that time was delivering coal to the miners who lived in the coal camp. I had finished early and was looking forward to getting home.

As I neared the road that led to my home, I was flagged down by my stepfather. He told me about a mother with three children who lived about six miles up in the mountains. Her husband had died several months previously, leaving her and the children destitute. In the tradition of taking care of our own, the miners had assembled several boxes of food, clothing, and gifts that they wanted me to deliver, along with a load of coal, to the family.

Now believe me, I didn't want to go. Let's face it, I had worked hard all day, it was Christmas Eve, and I wanted to get home to my family. But that was just it—it was Christmas Eve, the time of giving and goodwill. With this thought in mind, I turned the truck around and drove back to the coal tipple, where I filled the truck. When I returned, I loaded boxes in the front seat and in every nook and cranny I could find in the back. Then I set off.

Back in the hills of West Virginia, folks had built homes in some pretty out-of-the-way places. This woman's place was really out of the way. I had to travel on a road that had not been cleared by the highway department, nor had any path been made by traffic. I drove up the valley as I had been directed and turned off the road into a hollow called Lick Fork. The "road" was actually a snow-filled creek bed. When I saw that, I began to have doubts that I could make it. Nevertheless, I shifted into first gear and crept ahead.

When I came to the place a mile farther on where I was supposed to turn into the mountain to get to the woman's house, my heart dropped. There before me was a winding path that had been hand-cut up the side of the mountain. I still could not see her house. I pulled the truck up to the path and got out. After looking the situation over, I decided there was no way I could get that two-ton dump truck up through that path.

What am I to do? I wondered. Maybe I can just dump the coal and ask the family to come down for the food and clothes. So I got out and walked up the path. It was near dusk, the temperature had dropped, and the blowing snow was beginning to drift.

The path was about six feet wide, overhung with snow-covered branches and littered with stumps and limbs. Finally I reached the clearing where the house stood, a little shack with thin walls and cracks you could see through. I called the woman out of the house, explained why I was there, and asked if she had any way to carry the food and coal. She showed me a homemade wagon with wheelbarrow wheels.

Here I was in ten inches of snow, with a truck I had to empty before dark, an impassable path, and a wagon with wheelbarrow wheels. The only solution, as I could see it, was to turn the truck around, back it in as far as I could, dump the coal, and set the boxes off.

As I returned to the truck, I kept asking, "Lord, what am I doing here?"

I started up the engine, turned my old truck around, and went into reverse. Foot by foot that old truck backed up along that mountain path. I kept telling myself, "I'll just keep going until I can't go any farther."

However, the truck seemed to have a mind of its own. All at once, I was sitting there in the dark with my tail lights reflecting through the snow on that little shack. I was dumbfounded. That old truck had not slipped one inch or gotten stuck one time. And standing on the porch were four of the happiest people I had ever seen.

I unloaded the boxes and then dumped the coal, shoveling as much as I could under the sagging porch. As I worked, the thin, ill-clothed children dragged and pushed the boxes into the shack. When I had finished, the woman grasped my hand and thanked me over and over.

After the good-byes, I got into the truck and started back. Darkness had overtaken me. However, upon reaching the "road," I stopped the truck and looked back at the path. "There is no way," I said to myself, "that I could have maneuvered this truck up that mountain, through all that snow, in the dark, without help from somewhere."

I had been raised to worship God. I believed in the birth of Christ. And that Christmas Eve, in the hills of West Virginia, I knew I had been an instrument of what Christmas is all about.

Return *to* Bethlehem

It is more blessed to give than to receive.
−ACTS 20:35

WHEN CHRISTMAS PAST IS PRESENT

NORMAN VINCENT PEALE

My memories of Christmas around the turn of the century in the town of Lynchburg, Ohio, are still crystal clear. My father used to boost me up so I could crank my grandmother's doorbell, and everybody inside came running. I can smell the warm tallow of lighted candles on the tree and the aroma of homemade candy bubbling in a pot on the wood stove. It was a thrill to wake up and find an orange in my stocking, and I'll never forget how excited I was the year I got a banana! We were a country preacher's family, and we were poor. But we had a mighty good time.

One year my brother Bob and I dreamed of getting a bicycle. For months we haunted the stores looking at wheels and argued long about the color. At last we agreed: It had to be red.

Christmas morning we crept downstairs. There were small gifts under the tree—but no bicycle. Then Mother said to us, "Let's go down to the railroad station. Maybe Santa Claus forgot something, and perhaps it will come on the morning train."

So down we went to the old B&O station to meet the train. The door of the baggage car rolled open, and there it was—a bicycle with a light on the front. It was secondhand, and we boys had to share it, but it was ours and it was red! Later I learned that Mother had made her threadbare coat last yet another season so we might have our dreamed-of bicycle.

When I was seven or so, we lived in Cincinnati, close to the tracks where the streetcars screeched around corners. A special car came along to grease the rails, and we children, I'm sorry to say, made fun of the grimy old guy who ran it. "Greasy Dick," we shouted when he came by. "Hey, Greasy Dick!"

One day right before Christmas my father asked me to come along on one of his hospital calls. "Someone you will recognize isn't feeling well," he said. Propped up in a bed was Greasy Dick! My father introduced him by his real name, just as he would the finest gentleman, and when he shook my hand, it didn't feel greasy at all. "I hope you grow up to be a fine man like your father," he exclaimed. My father gave a prayer and patted his shoulder. When we left my father said, "Remember, Norman, he's not Greasy Dick; he's a friend of ours. And he's a child of God."

As I grew up, I came to appreciate what a precious gift Dad had given to me. He'd taught me to look for the good in people, always. It was a Christmas present that affected my whole life, and one I've always prayed I might pass on to others...

Once, a young lady from Switzerland, Ursula, lived with our family in New York City. As Christmas approached, she wondered what she could give us in gratitude.

She went to a children's shop, bought a beautiful baby dress, and had it gift wrapped. Then she approached one of the Salvation Army people on a corner. "Sir," she said, "I have a dress for a poor baby. Do you know of one?"

"More than one, I am afraid."

Together they hailed a cab and the Salvation Army man gave an address uptown. When the taxi pulled up in front of a rundown tenement, the Salvation Army officer took in the package. "Say it is from someone who has been blessed and wants to pass those blessings on," Ursula told him.

When the cab driver finally delivered Ursula back to our home, he told her there was no charge. "Don't worry," he said. "I've been more than paid for this." Ursula told us about her present on Christmas morning. It was one of the nicest we ever got.

After our three children grew up and had families of their own, there came a time when my wife, Ruth, and I found ourselves in London for the holidays. We were determined to have a Charles Dickens adventure. On Christmas Eve we had a hearty dinner and then went walking, our footsteps echoing in the deserted streets. It was gloomy going, and just about the time it seemed our Christmas spirits might never get off the ground, we heard singing from far away.

As we walked along, the sound of trumpeting brass and the chorus of jubilant voices got louder and louder. "O Come, All Ye Faithful!" "It Came Upon the Midnight Clear!" We heard them all. As we neared Trafalgar Square, we could see it was packed with thousands of people. A Salvation Army band was playing on a platform. It was bitter cold, but those people were having the time of their lives, singing "Joy to the World" at the top of their lungs.

There we were, so many miles from home, and yet right at home because of the spirit that surrounded us. We felt the same way several years ago when we took all our children and grandchildren on a trip to Africa and sat outside our tent under glittering stars as we read the story of the Nativity from the gospel of Luke.

There's a story about an African boy who gave his missionary-teacher an unusually beautiful seashell as a Christmas gift that's always meant a lot to Ruth and me. The boy had walked a great distance, over rough terrain, to the only place on the coast where these particular shells could be found. The teacher was touched. "You've traveled so far to bring me such a wonderful present," she said. The boy looked puzzled, then his eyes widened with excitement. "Oh, teacher," he explained, "long walk part of gift."

Sure, there have been plenty of times over the years when all the pre-holiday shopping and sermon writing and schedule arranging seemed to be too much, and my wife and I have been tempted to throw up our hands and say, "It's just not worth the effort!" But then we've looked at each other and said, "Long walk part of gift." And we've laughed and gotten back to work.

These stories are part of a golden thread that weaves us all together, strengthening us for the years ahead. Christmas is the ongoing affirmation of the greatest ideals and truth that anybody ever came up with. People feel reborn, invigorated, whole. Over and over, through the ages it goes.

Backward glances don't make me nostalgic and sad—not at all. They give me a burst of excitement for going forward. And they add to the richness of celebrating Christmas now.

*A prayer, in its simplest definition, is merely
a wish turned heavenward.*

—PHILLIPS BROOKS

MY CHRISTMAS MIRACLE

TAYLOR CALDWELL

For many of us, one Christmas stands out from all the others, the one when the meaning of the day shone clearest.

Although I did not guess it, my own "truest" Christmas began on a rainy spring day in the bleakest year of my life. Recently divorced, I was in my twenties, had no job, and was on my way downtown to go the rounds of the employment offices. I had no umbrella, for my old one had fallen apart, and I could not afford another one. I sat down in the streetcar, and there against the seat was a beautiful silk umbrella with a silver handle inlaid with gold and flecks of bright enamel. I had never seen anything so lovely.

I examined the handle and saw a name engraved among the golden scrolls. The usual procedure would have been to turn in the umbrella to the conductor, but on impulse I decided to take it with me and find the owner myself. I got off the streetcar in a downpour and thankfully opened the umbrella to protect myself. Then I searched a telephone book for the name on the umbrella and found it. I called, and a lady answered.

Yes, she said in surprise, that was her umbrella, which her parents, now dead, had given her for a birthday present. But, she added, it had been stolen from her locker at school (she was a teacher) more than a year before. She was so excited that I forgot I was looking for a job and went directly to her small house. She took the umbrella, and her eyes filled with tears.

The teacher wanted to give me a reward, but—though $20 was all I had in the world—her happiness at retrieving this special possession was such that to have accepted money would have spoiled something. We talked for a while, and I must have given her my address. I don't remember.

The next six months were wretched. I was able to obtain only temporary employment here and there, for a small salary, though this was what they now call the Roaring Twenties. But I put aside twenty-five or fifty cents when I could afford it for my little girl's Christmas presents. It took me six months to save $8. My last job ended the day before Christmas, my $30 rent was soon due, and I had $15 to my name—which Peggy and I would need for food. She was home from her convent boarding school and was excitedly looking forward to her gifts the next day, which I had already purchased. I had bought her a small tree, and we were going to decorate it that night.

The stormy air was full of the sound of Christmas merriment as I walked from the streetcar to my small apartment. Bells rang and children shouted in the bitter dusk of the evening; windows were lighted and everyone was running and laughing. But there would be no Christmas for me, I knew, no gifts, no remembrance whatsoever. As I struggled through the snowdrifts, I just about reached the lowest point in my life. Unless a miracle happened, I would be homeless in January, foodless, jobless. I had prayed steadily for weeks, and there had been no answer but this coldness and darkness, this harsh air, this abandonment. God and men had completely forgotten me. I felt old as death, and as lonely. What was to become of us?

I looked in my mailbox. There were only bills in it, a sheaf of them, and two white envelopes which I was sure contained more bills. I went up three dusty flights of stairs, and I cried, shivering in my thin coat. But I made myself smile so I could greet my little daughter with a pretense of happiness. She opened the door for me and threw herself in my arms, screaming joyously and demanding that we decorate the tree immediately.

Peggy was not yet six years old, yet had been alone all day while I worked. She had set our kitchen table for our evening meal, proudly, and put pans out and the three cans of food which would be our dinner. For some reason, when I looked at those pans and cans, I felt brokenhearted. We would have only hamburgers for our Christmas dinner tomorrow, and gelatin. I stood in the cold little kitchen, and misery overwhelmed me. For the first time in my life, I doubted the existence of God and His mercy, and the coldness in my heart was colder than ice.

The doorbell rang, and Peggy ran fleetly to answer it, calling that it must be Santa Claus. Then I heard a man talking heartily to her and went to the door. He was a delivery man, his arms were full of big parcels, and he was laughing at my child's frenzied joy and her dancing. "This is a mistake," I said, but he read the name on the parcels, and they were for me. When he had gone I could only stare at the boxes. Peggy and I sat on the floor and opened them. A huge doll, three times the size of the one I had bought for her. Gloves. Candy. A beautiful leather purse. Incredible! I looked for the name of the sender. It was the teacher, the address simply "California," where she had moved.

Our dinner that night was the most delicious I had ever eaten. I could only pray in myself, "Thank You, Father." I forgot I had no money for the rent and only $15 in my purse and no job. My child and I ate and laughed together in happiness. Then we decorated the little tree and marveled at it. I put Peggy to bed and set up her gifts around the tree, and a sweet peace flooded me like a benediction. I had some hope again. I could even examine the sheaf of bills without cringing. Then I opened the two white envelopes. One contained a check for $30 from a company I had worked for briefly in the summer. It was, said a note, my "Christmas bonus." My rent!

The other envelope was an offer of a permanent position with the government—to begin two days after Christmas. I sat with the letter in my hand and the check on the table before me, and I think that was the most joyful moment of my life up to that time.

The church bells began to ring. I hurriedly looked at my child, who was sleeping blissfully, and ran down to the street. Everywhere people were walking to church to celebrate the birth of the Saviour. People smiled at me and I smiled back. The storm had stopped; the sky was pure and glittering with stars.

"The Lord is born!" sang the bells to the crystal night and the laughing darkness. Someone began to sing, "Come, all ye faithful!" I joined in and sang with the strangers all about me.

I am not alone at all, I thought. *I was never alone at all*.

And that, of course, is the message of Christmas. We are never alone. Not when the night is darkest, the wind coldest, the world seemingly most indifferent. For this is still the time God chooses.

*A coincidence is a small miracle where God
chose to remain anonymous.*

−HEIDE QUADE

HOLY LAND HOLIDAY

BETTY McCONOUGHEY

My husband, Jim, and I had looked forward to this trip for a long time. We had arrived in Jerusalem one day early for a two-week tour of Israel in November 1995. I was especially looking forward to going to Bethlehem. What better way to prepare for Christmas than to visit the birthplace of Jesus?

Our hotel was inside the Old City walls, where most of Jerusalem's biblical sites are located. We wouldn't venture as far as Bethlehem on our own. Not without a guide. "Let's go to the Western Wall," Jim said.

We got there during a bar mitzvah. A tall wooden fence separated men and women, so mothers stood on chairs to watch this traditional celebration of a son's passage to manhood. Prayers on bits of paper were tucked into cracks between stones worn smooth from centuries of being touched. I put my fingers to the cool wall and asked God to keep us safe.

On the way back to the hotel we followed a walkway that led to a steep flight of steps. At the top we stopped to catch our breath and snap a picture of the glimmering Dome of the Rock, then trudged on and ended up in the Jewish Quarter.

"I need something to drink, and I need to sit down!" Jim said with uncharacteristic impatience. I looked at him, surprised by his agitation. Something wasn't right. We walked until we found an outdoor cafe, where Jim drank a bottle of water. "It's my chest," he said. "It feels tight." *Please, God, don't let it be a heart attack*, I prayed.

After sitting for a while we made our way to the nearest taxi stand. A driver pulled up almost immediately, but he refused to take us. Did he not want to get involved, with Jim looking so sick? By the time a second taxi stopped at the curb, Jim was having trouble breathing. "I know where to take him," the driver assured me.

We arrived at the emergency room before noon and waited all day for test results. The doctors decided Jim should stay overnight, and Jim insisted I go back to the hotel. "Your husband is in good hands," the nurse informed me; we had been delivered to a teaching hospital that specialized in heart problems.

On my way out, I stopped at the lobby pay phone to check in with the tour director. The phone only took cards, and though a card-dispensing machine was nearby, I didn't have the right shekels to use it. I pressed my hand to my forehead, not sure if I could handle another problem. A man sitting across the way offered to help. He gave me the correct change and showed me how the card worked. Still another obstacle: the tour director had left for the day. It seemed as if the world was collapsing around me.

Back in the hotel room I sat on the edge of the bed and unhooked my money belt. It was empty! My passport, traveler's checks, and shekels were not inside! I mentally retraced my path. I had paid the cab driver with money from my purse and couldn't remember the last time I had gone into the belt. I jumped up to start searching when the missing items fell to the floor. I had forgotten to rezip the belt, but luckily its contents had been caught in my clothing. How long had I been walking around like that?

Exhausted, I lay on the bed, ready to leave if the hospital called. *Lord, we've come all this way to see your birthplace at Christmastime. Why this?*

The words seemed to form in my head, *"Rest in me. I have gone ahead of you and removed every stone."*

I didn't understand. Hadn't God overlooked a big stone? Jim was in the hospital! And we had had a day full of lesser hassles. I still hadn't forgotten about the taxi that refused to pick us up when we were in such desperate need.

Of course, the other taxi had taken us to the perfect hospital…And I was grateful for the kind gentleman who had helped me with the phone. And thank goodness the items from my money belt had stayed in my clothing! *Were all of these coincidences,* I wondered suddenly, *or stones removed?*

The next morning I returned to the hospital, and the doctors had a firm diagnosis: Jim had suffered a mild heart attack. I drifted to the waiting room to pull myself together. I looked out over the buildings of Jerusalem and remembered the words from the night before: Rest in me. It was a promise I would have to trust.

Jim and I dropped out of the tour and spent two weeks in a hotel above the Hinnom Valley on Mount Zion while he recuperated enough to make the trip home. Each day we strolled through the garden, where grapevines and olive trees grew and pomegranates ripened. Evenings we watched the sun set over the city. We rested and prayed, and felt Christ's constant presence.

At Christmastime so much of my attention had always been on the baby Jesus. But being so close to Bethlehem—and not getting to it—made me realize that, like the boys we had seen bar mitzvahed, Jesus too had become a man. We celebrate Christmas not just because he was born, but because he lives today. I had seen him in a taxi driver, a kind stranger, and in the "coincidences" prepared for us from the moment we arrived. I came home that year without setting foot in Bethlehem, but better prepared for Christmas than I had ever imagined.

*Faith in yourself and faith in God are
the key to mastery of fear.*
−HAROLD SHERMAN

THE LITTLE SHEPHERD'S GIFT

DRUE DUKE

Jonathan, shoulders drooping, peered down the long slope of the hill into the darkness where his brothers had disappeared. His nostrils quivered with disappointment. How he wanted to go with them!

"I want to see the Baby, too," he had pleaded.

"The sheep can't be left unattended," his eldest brother said firmly. "You are the youngest; you must stay with them."

It would have done no good to tell them he was afraid a wolf might attack the flock while they were gone. They would only laugh and remind him that he was afraid of everything. Having six older brothers was not easy. They ordered him about and they teased him because he couldn't do many things they did. If only he had their courage; if he weren't afraid all the time! Tonight, when the big star appeared and the angels came, he was terrified.

But even his brothers seemed so frightened then that one angel said, "Fear not," and told them about the wonderful Baby: and all the angels sang a beautiful song, "Glory to God in the highest, and on earth peace, good will toward men."

When the angels left, his brothers gathered up the finest new lambs to take as a gift to the Baby. And they set out, leaving Jonathan alone.

The fire burned low and Jonathan threw some more sticks on it. The night was less fearful with a big fire glowing. He wrapped his robe about him, sat down on the ground, and looked up at the big star. He must not go to sleep. He closed his eyes just so he could see in his memory the beautiful angels and hear their singing…

"Jonathan!" His name was being called. Jonathan sprang to his feet. One of the angels stood over him. The boy cringed in fear, but the man with the shining face smiled and said, "Fear not. I, too, bring good news. The Lord heard you say you wanted to see the Baby, and He sent me to take you to Him."

"Oh, but I cannot leave the sheep. There will be no one to watch them."

"Your sheep will be safe," the angel said. "I promise you. Tonight the greatest Shepherd ever is present."

"I don't understand…" Jonathan began.

"It isn't necessary that you understand. Just trust me."

There was something about the angel that made all of Jonathan's fear melt away. He reached out and took the strong hand offered him.

And then an amazing thing happened. The fire and the sheep and the hillside seemed to disappear. Only the star remained. Jonathan had a sensation of moving, and something—or someone—held him fast.

When the moving stopped, it took a few moments for him to adjust his eyes to the dim surroundings. The star's brilliance was gone, and the smell of cattle and hay permeated the air. Jonathan was standing in a cave, the kind used as a stable.

And there was the Baby, lying in a manger! A beautiful woman sat beside Him. On the straw-covered floor knelt his brothers and some other shepherds and three men in handsome robes who offered the Baby gifts in golden boxes.

Jonathan turned frightened eyes on the angel. "My brothers will be very angry that I am here," he whispered.

"They cannot see you or hear you while you are with me."

Jonathan frowned slightly. "I wish I had something to give the Baby," he murmured.

"You do."

"No." He shook his head sadly and held out his empty hands. "I have nothing."

The angel bent very close to him. "Jonathan, what is your deepest desire?" he whispered. "Don't you long to be strong and unafraid, as your brothers are?"

"Oh, yes, I do!"

"Tell Him. Give Him your heart and its desire. He will fill your heart with His love and take away your fears. That is what He was born for."

As Jonathan stared at the manger, the Baby turned His head and looked straight at him. Warmth flooded Jonathan's body, and he knelt on the straw.

"I have nothing to bring you, little Baby," he whispered, "except me. But here I am. I give you my heart and all my fears."

The Baby smiled directly at Jonathan, and the boy felt his shoulders rise, his back straighten, his chin lift.

Eyes wide, he raised his face toward the angel and said, "I won't be afraid again."

Jonathan turned to look again at the Baby, but He was gone. The stable, his brothers, the richly-dressed men, even the angel—all gone. In their place were the hillside, the sleeping sheep, the embers of a campfire, and overhead, the wonderful star.

"Was it a dream?" Jonathan muttered, getting up from the ground. "Did I fall asleep and dream it all?"

But as he stood and felt the straightness of his back, the sense of boldness that filled him, the warm glow in his heart, he knew it was no dream.

He stretched his arms high and raised his eyes toward heaven.

"Thank you, God," he said, "for sending the angel. I know that tonight I saw the Holy Baby."

And his brothers, coming back up the hillside, heard his voice, full of confidence, ringing clear, "Glory to God in the highest. Amen! Amen!"

The greatest happiness in the world is to make others happy.
–LUTHER BURBANK

O LITTLE TOWN

NANCY SCHRAFFENBERGER

Many years passed before I was old enough to understand why my young parents had worked such long hours in the chilly dimness of the carriage barn, oiling leather and rusty hinges, sanding splintered wood, waxing dull metal. But I know now that they were drawn by a sense of the rising magic of Christmas Eve, to make a necessary journey…

On December 24th, in the Depression year 1937, a vast white blanket, thick and rumpled, covered the fields in the Mohawk Valley. Across the frozen river from the farmhouse where my grandmother and I stood at a window, the lights of the very small village glistened like a handful of stars scattered in the snow.

"It's a fine clear night," my grandmother said. "The folks over there won't have any trouble getting to the midnight service." I looked up into her face and saw her faded-blue eyes focused longingly on the little village church steeple that rose above the rooftops far across the drifted snow on the other side of the river, pointing to the sky in the shape of praying hands.

She sighed, then let the curtain fall over the window; we turned back to the glow of the kerosene lamps lighting the parlor. "It's time to get the crèche ready, Nancy," she said, lifting down a wooden box from the top of the piano. "Soon Baby Jesus will be here."

My parents and I were staying with my grandmother in the old family homestead that winter when I was four. Instead of closing the house and renting a room in the city for the cold months, as she normally did, Grandma had invited us to move in with her—three miles out in the country—until my father could find work and we could afford to live on our own.

The isolated house was an antique—150 years old, with no electricity and only the most primitive heating and plumbing. But we were cozy there. We ate, worked, and socialized in the big warm kitchen and slept near Franklin stoves in the back parlor and dining room. The root cellar was heaped high, and rows of gleaming Mason jars displayed jewel-like contents—emerald peas, ruby tomatoes, golden peaches and such—canned the previous summer. Occasionally, people brought my father mechanical repairs to do; my mother and grandmother had a kind of cottage industry, making braided rugs that were sold by a city department store.

Our only lack, really, was transportation. My grandmother's automobile was permanently parked in the barn alongside broken-down wagons and carriages; there was no money for gasoline. During mild weather we could row across the river to the village on the opposite shore to attend church and buy necessities at the general store. But when the snow fell and the river froze and the razor-edged winds came slicing down the valley, only my father made that trip, by foot, and only to replenish vital food supplies.

It was not getting to church services that was a real hardship for Grandma. After her husband died and, one by one, her six children moved away, the congregation had become her family. There she had taught Sunday school, played the organ, laundered the altar cloths; she had brought home-made biscuits and preserves for new mothers, homegrown flowers for the shut-in and bereaved.

By Christmas Eve, Grandma hadn't seen her church or her church family for almost three months. Though she longed to welcome Jesus in God's House, she knew this was not possible. Now she and I carefully laid out the manger scene on the parlor mantelpiece. While we worked, my parents came in from the mysterious business that had occupied them off and on for the past few weeks. We ate an early supper and then gathered around Grandma at the piano to sing carols. Afterward I remember the feeling of closeness and love as I was passed from lap to lap while the grownups took turns reading the Christmas scriptures in Matthew and Luke. At some point I must have fallen asleep and been put to bed. And some time after that my parents must have told Grandma about their Christmas gift to her.

My first knowledge of it was my mother's urgent whisper, "Wake up, Nancy, there's a surprise." She tugged my leggings and heavy sweater on over my flannel nightgown and wrapped me in my quilt. Then my father came in and picked me up, a fat patchwork bundle, and carried me out of the front door. Waiting in front of the porch steps was a box sleigh filled with straw and hitched to it a pair of huge mules as tall as houses. My grandmother was already seated in the back, wreathed in a tapestry of quilts, regal as a queen. My father tucked me in next to her and she drew me close. Spellbound, I watched him help my mother up on the bench seat and climb up beside her.

"All set?" he asked, looking over his shoulder. "Gee up, Buck, gee up, Bright!" He cracked the reins smartly on the mules' backs and the great creatures set their hooves, then leaned into their harnesses. With a lurch, the sleigh moved forward, snow squeaking under its runners. It moved jerkily at first, then more smoothly as the mules settled in to a stride. The cold air was like a sparkling tonic I could taste. Above, the arching night sky was scribbled with silver constellations; the world around us was a darkened amphitheater filled with breathless, motionless waiting.

My father guided the sleigh around the rutted driveway to the back of the house, over the snow-covered garden and down the incline to the cove where we docked the rowboat in the summer. Then we were on the river ice, marble white and marble solid, the mules stepping securely, the harness bells jingling like a pocketful of coins.

"Grandma," I whispered, "where are we going?" I looked up into her face, as carved and keen as an old shepherd's.

She gazed back at me, and in the crystalline moonlight I could see her eyes. They were starred with happiness.

"To Bethlehem," she said.

He that hath no cross deserves no crown.

−FRANCIS QUARLES

THREE SYMBOLS OF CHRISTMAS

BILLY GRAHAM

There are three symbols which mean Christmas—the real meaning of Christmas.

The first is the *cradle*. In words so familiar to us all, the Bible describes God in human flesh! In the person of a tiny infant! There, in Bethlehem, were cradled the hopes and dreams of a dying world. Those chubby little hands that clasped the straw in His manger crib were soon to open blind eyes, unstop deaf ears, and still the troubled seas. Those tiny feet were to take Him to the sick and needy and were to be pierced on Calvary's cross.

That manger crib in remote Bethlehem became the link that bound a lost world to a loving God.

The *cross*. There were both light and shadow on that first Christmas. There was joy with overtones of sadness, for Jesus was born to die. Jesus, approaching the cross, said, *To this end was I born, and for this cause came I into the world.* To Christians the joy of Christmas is not limited to His birth. It was His death and resurrection that gave meaning to His birth.

It is in the cross that the world can find a solution to its pressing problems.

The *crown*. Jesus was crowned with a crown of thorns and enthroned on a cruel cross, yet His assassins did something, perhaps unwittingly. They placed a superscription over His cross in Greek, Latin, and Hebrew: "This is the King."

Yes, Christ is King of kings and Lord of lords, and He is coming back someday. He will come not as a babe in Bethlehem's manger. The next time He comes it will be in a blaze of glory and He will be crowned Lord of all.

Cradle—cross—crown. Let them speak to you. Let the power of Him who came to us at Christmas grip you, and He will surely change your life.

The highest courage is to dare to appear to be what one is.
–JOHN LANCASTER SPALDING

IN ANOTHER STABLE

DAVID NIVEN

t took place on Christmas Eve 1939. I had just arrived in England from Hollywood to volunteer for the British Army. Having had some previous military experience, I was commissioned a second lieutenant and given command of a platoon. We were about to be sent to France and no one was very happy about it. Most of the men had been conscripted from good civilian jobs; this was the "phony war" period before the big German attack of the following spring, and it all seemed a big waste of time to most of them.

Being commanded by a Hollywood actor was an additional irritant for them and made the whole thing seem even more ridiculous. The men were not mutinous—but they were certainly forty of the least well-disposed characters I have ever been associated with, let alone been in command of.

We were not permitted liberty on that Christmas Eve because we were due to leave England and our families the next day—a fine prospect for the holidays. The entire platoon was billeted in the shabby stables of a farm near Dover.

I could sense the hostility in every soldier. The air was thick with sarcastic cracks about my bravery in various motion pictures.

It so happens that every night of my life I have knelt down by my bed and said a simple prayer. But that night I was faced with a difficult decision. If I suddenly knelt in prayer, here in front of these men, it occurred to me that forty tough soldiers would take it as a final evidence of Hollywood flamboyance.

On the other hand, I have always felt it wrong to avoid saying my prayers because the situation was not convenient. Besides, here it was the eve of Christ's birth.

Finally I summoned up my courage and knelt by my bunk.

As I prayed, there was some snickering at first, but it soon died away.

When I finished and lay down on the straw, I looked rather sheepishly around the stable and saw at least a dozen soldiers kneeling quietly and praying in their own way.

It was not the first time God had entered a stable—and touched the hearts of men.

For it is in giving that we receive.
–ST. FRANCIS OF ASSISI

CHRISTMAS IS ALWAYS

DALE EVANS ROGERS

Christmas was not just a starlit night in Bethlehem: it had been behind the stars forever.

There was Christmas in the heart of God when He made the earth, and then gave it away—to us. When He sent us His prophets, that was Christmas too. And it was the most magnificent Christmas of all that night in Bethlehem when He gave us His own son.

As Jesus grew up, Christmas was everywhere He went, in giving food, giving sight, giving life. For Christmas is giving.

But Christmas is also receiving. In the Bible it says: "*As many as received him, to them gave He power to become the sons of God...*"*

As many as received Him! When we understand that, we understand that receiving can be even more important than giving—at Christmas! When we receive Christ, we experience completely the gift that is Christmas.

Then, for us, Christmas is truly always, for Jesus said, "*Lo, I am with you always....*"**

And Christmas is Jesus!

*John 1:12   ** Matthew 28:20

The true spirit of Christmas is an angel's song sung by living Christ's example all year long.
—AUTHOR UNKNOWN

THE LOST MELODY

NORMAN VINCENT PEALE

At Christmastime I like to recall an old legend about the shepherds to whom the angels came. These men were sitting about their fire one evening, trying to remember the music that they had heard on the beautiful night of our Saviour's birth. The melody had been bright as a spring morning, sweet as the laughter of a child, but no one could sing or even hum it.

Suddenly, as they talked, they heard a faint bleating far up the hillside. At first no one moved. Each man knew that a lamb was in trouble, but the dangers of the darkness—the treacherousness of the rocky hillside or the chances of an encounter with wolves—held them frozen. Then, the youngest of the shepherds, little more than a boy, sprang to his feet and disappeared.

When he returned some time later, he was bruised and bleeding from slipping among the jagged rocks. But he held a little lamb safely in his arms.

"The strangest thing happened!" the young shepherd said exultantly. "On the way back, for no reason that I know, music seemed to fill my mind."

And then, while the other shepherds gaped in awe, he sang to them the lost melody.

Years passed. The Babe born at Bethlehem grew to manhood and was known far and wide as a great prophet. One day, so the legend goes, His followers came to Him and said, "Master, there is a blind man who stops often at the gates, tells stories to children, and sings a melody of great beauty. Won't You come and hear him?"

So Jesus went and listened to the sweetness of the blind man's song. Then, gently, Jesus touched His finger to the man's eyes.

The singer leaped to his feet, crying, "I see. I see again!" And looking upon Jesus, he asked in wonder, "Who are you?"

Jesus must have smiled. "We have met before—long ago. Do you remember when you first heard that melody?"

Then the man told Jesus about the night he rescued the little lamb.

"Yes," replied the Master. "It is given to many men to hear that refrain from My Father's choir; but all too few learn to keep it alive, as you have done, with a loving heart and kindly deeds."

*In the sphere of material things, giving means being rich.
Not he who has much is rich, but he who gives much.*

—ERICH FROMM

A WAY TO MAKE CHRISTMAS
MORE MEANINGFUL

CATHERINE MARSHALL

At Thanksgiving time several years ago, the question came up in one of our family sessions: How could the coming Christmas be made more meaningful? And it was the children who, as usual, went right to the heart of the matter: We had to find some way to think more about others.

"I think we should find a poor family and help them," said Jeff, our youngest. It was a good idea—but which poor family? Then one of us happened to mention the Stowes (not their real name), and instantly we were all excited. Actually the Stowes were not poverty-stricken; Mr. Stowe was a schoolteacher, but as such he symbolized to us all those respected citizens who serve selflessly and often with small pay. The Stowes had five children; they lived in a house much too small for such a large family; they were always to be counted on for community projects; and yet they never had those "extras" that many people take for granted.

"Could we give a present to each one?" Chester asked.

"At least," said Linda. "Maybe several."

"Clothes?" suggested Jeff, though actually he had toys and food more clearly in mind.

It was my husband, Len, who suggested that the Stowes not be told where the proposed gift came from. Len was thinking of the theme of Lloyd Douglas' *The Magnificent Obsession*, of the power that flows from giving anonymously.

That very day we gave ourselves research assignments. There was detective work to be done on clothing sizes, on the particular wishes and fancies of the five Stowe children. We set up a large cardboard box in the living room; and gradually, as Christmas neared, the box began to fill with presents. For Mrs. Stowe I bought a silk slip, lingerie I suspected she would never treat herself to; and without telling me, Len had a similar idea for Mr. Stowe—a handsome sport shirt. Gently, ever so reverently, the boys placed their own special gifts in the box—baseballs autographed by their particular major-league idols. So it went—clothes and games, toys and eats, personal treasures right up to the top.

Last of all came one of the few anonymous letters I have ever written. In it I explained to the Stowes that the point of the gifts was to try to say to them what their own unselfish giving meant to one family, as well as to others in the community.

Then on Christmas Eve came the most exciting time of all. Our whole family climbed into the station wagon and drove to the Stowes', where furtively, breathlessly, with a Halloween kind of fun, we left the box on the Stowe doorstep and cut out—but fast—for home!

I have marveled at how the excitement of giving can transform the atmosphere in our home to thoughtfulness, consideration, love, self-sacrifice. Since that first year we tried a project together, I have heard of many other families who find similar rewards in coordinated family giving. Some friends in New York invite an orphan home for the holidays every year; a family in Wisconsin makes toys for a children's hospital one year and "adopts" the lonely people in a retirement home the next.

When Miami, Florida, began to swell with Cubans fleeing from Castro, a family there devoted its Christmas to caring for a refugee family. Each year they choose their Christmas project keeping in mind the urgent community needs.

Every year as Christmas seems to come faster than ever, every year when that glorious event catches us all but unprepared for its surge of warmth and generosity, I am convinced that a family project can add a new dimension to family solidarity and new emphasis to what the Babe of Bethlehem means to the world.

*Give what you have. To some one, it may be
better than you dare to think.*

—HENRY WADSWORTH LONGFELLOW

UNEXPECTED CHRISTMAS

MARGUERITE NIXON

We were well over halfway to our farm in East Texas when the storm broke. Lightning flashed, thunder crashed, and a tree fell with a great ripping noise. When the rain poured in such a flood that we could not see the road, my husband drove off on to what seemed to be a bit of clearing deep in the piney woods.

As we waited, I sensed we would not get to the farm that night to celebrate Christmas Eve with our family. We were sitting there, miserable and dejected, when I heard a knocking on my window. A man with a lantern stood there beckoning us to follow him. My husband and I splashed after him up the path to his house.

A woman with a lamp in her hand stood in the doorway of an old house; a boy of about twelve and a little girl stood beside her. We went in soaked and dripping, and the family moved aside in order that we might have the warmth of the fire. With the volubility of city people, my husband and I began to talk, explaining our plans. And with the quietness of people who live in the silence of the woods, they listened.

"The bridge on Caney Creek is out. You are welcome to spend the night with us," the man said. And though we told them we thought it was an imposition, especially on Christmas Eve, they insisted. After we had visited a while longer, the man got up and took the Bible from the mantel. "It's our custom to read the story from St. Luke on Christmas Eve," he said, and without another word he began:

And she brought forth her firstborn Son, and wrapped Him in swaddling clothes, and laid Him in a manger....

The children sat up eagerly, their eyes bright in anticipation, while their father read on: *And there were in the same country shepherds abiding in the field, keeping watch over their flocks by night.* I looked at his strong face. He could have been one of them.

When he finished reading and closed the Bible, the little children knelt by their chairs. The mother and father were kneeling, and without any conscious will of my own I found myself joining them. Then I saw my husband, without any embarrassment at all, kneel also.

When we arose, I looked around the room. There were no bright-wrapped packages or cards, only a small, unadorned holly tree on the mantel. Yet the spirit of Christmas was never more real to me.

The little boy broke the silence. "We always feed the cattle at twelve o'clock on Christmas Eve. Come with us."

The barn was warm and fragrant with the smell of hay and dried corn. A cow and a horse greeted us, and there was a goat with a tiny, woolly kid that came up to be petted. This is like the stable where the Baby was born, I thought. Here is the manger, and the gentle animals keep watch.

When we returned to the house, there was an air of festivity and the serving of juice and fruitcake. Later, we bedded down on a mattress made of corn shucks. As I turned into a comfortable position, they rustled under me and sent up a faint fragrance exactly like that in the barn. My heart said, "You are sleeping in the stable like the Christ Child did."

As I drifted into a profound sleep, I knew that the light coming through the old pine shutters was the Star shining on that quiet house.

The family all walked down the path to the car with us the next morning. I was so filled with the Spirit of Christmas they had given me that I could find no words. Suddenly I thought of the gifts in the back seat of our car for our family.

I began to hand them out. My husband's gray woolen socks went to the man. The red sweater I had bought for my sister went to his wife. I gave away two boxes of candy, the white mittens, and the leather gloves while my husband nodded approval.

And when I was breathless from reaching in and out of the car and the family stood there loaded with the gaiety of Christmas packages, the mother spoke for all of them. "We thank you," she said simply. And then she said, "Wait."

She hurried up the path to the house and came back with a quilt folded across her arms. It was beautifully handmade; the pattern was the Star of Bethlehem. I looked up at the tall beautiful pines because my throat hurt and I could not speak. It was indeed Christmas.

Every Christmas Eve since then, I sleep under that quilt, the Star of Bethlehem; and in my memory I visit the stable and smell again the corn shucks, and the meaning of Christmas abides with me once more.

A Christmas "miracle" brings the joy of God among us and calms a troubled spirit.
—JULIE K. LUNENSCHLOSS

THE BABE OF BETHLEHEM

DORIS SWEHLA

Phyllis wasn't an easy child to love. I wanted the best for her and I prayed for God to bless her, but sometimes I did wish she wasn't in the particular Sunday school class I taught. Phyllis had stringy hair, dirty fingernails, and a runny nose. She kept apart from the rest of the children and she walked with a sort of stomp. Besides that, she never sat still, she hated to be touched, and she always had to have the last word.

I was twenty years old, and that year I supervised my first Christmas program at the big old stone church, Tabernacle Baptist, on Chicago's West Side. Early in Advent I held the typed pages of the Nativity script in my hand as I stood before the assembled children.

"If you'd like a speaking part in the program, raise your hand," I said, and almost every hand shot up. Not Phyllis's, of course. When everyone who wanted a part had one, I still had a few left.

"Phyllis," I said, "wouldn't you like just a few words to say in the program?"

"Who said I was coming to your program?" she asked, arms folded across her chest and chair tipped precariously on its back legs. "I'm probably going to a party that night," she said grandly.

Lord, I prayed silently, *please help me love Phyllis.*

"Well, I do have a few more parts if you change your mind."

"I won't," Phyllis said, and she didn't.

On dress rehearsal afternoon, the children sat in the darkened front pews of the church, whispering to each other as the adults put final touches on the bath towel headdresses of the shepherds and the tinsel halos of the angels.

"Okay, take your places," I called from the back of the sanctuary. The reader began: "In those days, there went out a decree..." A shiver rippled over me. Again I was immersed in the age-old story.

"Mary doesn't act like she's gonna have a baby," muttered a husky little voice behind me. Phyllis might not have any desire to be in the program, but she wouldn't miss the rehearsal!

"Shhhh!" I whispered, reaching back to pat Phyllis's hand. She jerked it away, saying, "Okay! Okay!"

In the last scene, only a spotlight shone on the holy family, and the children hummed "Silent Night." It was beautiful—but who was that moving in front of the manger? Phyllis! You never knew where that child was going to pop up next. Now she stuck her hand into the manger, squeezed the doll's arm, and disappeared back into the shadows.

"Phyllis," I called, "what are you doing up there?"

"I'm just looking," she said. "Besides, it's not a baby. It's just a doll. I felt it."

Lord, please help me love Phyllis.

"All right," I said to the cast. "Everyone be here at six-thirty so that you'll be in costume and ready to start promptly at seven. See you tonight."

Phyllis stomped up the aisle with the rest of the departing children. *With any luck at all*, I thought, *she will have had enough this afternoon and won't be back tonight.* I knew this wasn't a Christian reaction, but I did want the program to go smoothly.

By 6:45, the air was bristling with excitement backstage. Angels helped drape each other's bedsheet robes. Joseph and the wise men adjusted the beard wires that hooked over their ears. Mary stared into the mirror trying to capture just the right look for the mother of the Savior. I moved from group to group, helping where I could. There was no Phyllis to be seen and I began to relax.

Just a minute before seven, Mrs. Wright entered. In her arms she held her tiny new baby. All wrapped in white, he would replace the doll we'd used in rehearsals. "He's just been fed," she said, "so he should sleep during the program."

"You can put him in the manger just as the lights go down," I whispered.

As the organ chimed the beginning of the service, I took my prompter's seat in the front pew. With the opening strains of "Watchman, Tell Us of the Night," the lights came up on the manger scene, and the narrator began.

But instead of the familiar shiver as I heard the beginning of the Christmas scripture, I felt something bump my knee and give a little shove. "Move over," muttered an all-too-familiar voice. "I decided not to go to the party."

Not taking my eyes from the drama unfolding up front, I moved over and reached out to pat Phyllis's knee. She flung my hand back into my lap.

I'm trying, Lord, I thought.

The angels sang to the shepherds. The shepherds went to Bethlehem and took a lamb for the baby. The wise men went to see Herod and then to the stable. And Mary sat there "pondering these things in her heart." It was lovely. Phyllis sat beside me so quietly that I forgot all about her, and when I realized she was gone, it was too late.

She stomped her way right up to the manger, just as she had done during the rehearsal. But this time she stiffened, awe-struck, then turned, eyes wide with wonder, and came hurrying back to me.

"He's alive!" she said to me in a penetrating whisper.

Across the aisle, someone asked, "What did she say?"

"She said, 'He's alive!'"

Like ripples in a pond, the word passed from pew to pew, all the way to the back of the sanctuary. "He's alive ... alive ... alive." The air grew electric as one by one the people in the congregation felt the living presence of the Baby in Bethlehem.

Here was the real reason we all were celebrating. He's alive! Emmanuel— God with us, God incarnate. A tough, unruly little girl had brought the majestic Christmas message home. *God is alive!*

The lights came up, and when we stood to sing "Joy to the World! the Lord Is Come," the sound rocked our big old church as never before.

I put my arm around Phyllis's tight little shoulders. "You were the best part of the program," I said into her ear, drawing her close to my side.

"I wasn't in your program," she said. But she didn't push me away.

Example is not the main thing in influencing others.
It is the only thing.
—ALBERT SCHWEITZER

THE SPIRIT OF BETHLEHEM

CECIL B. DEMILLE

*D*uring this festive Christmas season, churches all over the country will overflow with worshipers. It wasn't always that way. . . .

When I was a boy of ten, our community church, in order to stimulate interest among parishioners, decided to hold services every morning at 8 A.M. for a week. Since we couldn't afford a resident minister, one was acquired from the outside. I do not remember his name. But I shall never forget his strong, kindly face and his prominent red beard.

My father, who was very active in the church, sent me off one cold and rainy morning. I walked alone to the small, wooden sanctuary through a murky gloom. Upon arriving, I could see that no one was present but the red-bearded minister and me.

I was the congregation.

Embarrassed, I took a seat, wondering anxiously what he would do. The hour for the service arrived. Surely he would tell me politely to run along home.

With calm and solemn dignity the minister walked into the pulpit. Then he looked down on me and smiled—a smile of great warmth and sincerity. In the congregation sat a solitary child, but he commenced the service as if the church were crowded to the walls.

A ritual opened the services, followed by a reading lesson to which I gave the responses. Then the minister preached a short sermon. He talked earnestly to me—and to God. When it came time for the offering, he placed the collection plate on the altar railing. I walked up and dropped my nickel into the plate.

Then he did a beautiful thing. He came down to the altar to receive my offering. As he did this, he placed his hand on my head. I can still feel the thrill and sensation of his gentle touch. It won my belief and strengthened my faith. The spirit of truth was in the church with us that morning.

None of us can tell at what moment we step into a boy's life and by a demonstration of love and faith turn him in God's direction.

Where your treasure is, there will your heart be also.
—MATTHEW 6:21

MAY WE KEEP IT IN OUR HEARTS

PETER MARSHALL

In a world that seems not only to be changing, but even to be dissolving, there are some tens of millions of us who want Christmas to be the same...

with the same old greeting "Merry Christmas" and no other.

We long for the abiding love among men of good will which the season brings...

believing in this ancient miracle of Christmas with its softening, sweetening influence to tug at our heart strings once again.

We want to hold on to the old customs and traditions because they strengthen our family ties, bind us to our friends, make us one with all mankind for whom the Child was born, and bring us back again to the God Who gave His only begotten Son, that "whosoever believeth in Him should not perish, but have everlasting life."

So we will not "spend" Christmas...

nor "observe" Christmas.

We will "keep" Christmas—keep it as it is...

in all the loveliness of its ancient traditions.

May we keep it in our hearts,

that we may be kept in its hope.

Memories & Moments

Behold, how good and how pleasant it is for brethren to dwell together in unity.

—PSALM 133:1

A FAMILY TIME

DEVITA CAIN WIDMER

Jason, our firstborn, was four months old that Christmas 1980. My husband, Steve, was in the Army, stationed in Bad Aibling, West Germany. It was our third year there, but the sadness of being away from home seemed worse than ever.

We'd just come back from a trip to Indiana to see Steve's father, who was dying, and had introduced Jason to my mom and dad back in North Carolina. After this time of closeness with our families, the return to Germany was hard, especially when word came that Steve's father had died. As Christmas drew nearer, I could not seem to fight the gloom I felt. Most of all, I missed the bustling of a large family. I was used to two turkeys and a ham with all the trimmings, and thirty relatives packed into one small house on Christmas Day. I wanted my young son to be part of that, to have those thirty people fussing over my baby, cuddling him, making him feel welcome and secure in this world.

Then came a call from Jason's godfather, Don Kraus, who was stationed at the Army base in Würzburg. Did we want company for Christmas? Of course we did! Don arrived two days before Christmas, bearing gifts, food, and a determination to make the holiday more cheerful for us.

He had a plan for Christmas Eve. We'd drive to a small village in Austria called Oberndorf, where "Silent Night" was composed and first sung on Christmas Eve, 1818. "We'll go to midnight Mass," Don said. "It will take several hours to get there. But I promise you it will be worth it."

As we set off that evening, all the world was white and smelled of pine and cedar. We drove in the dark, through the Alps, into Austria, and when we reached Oberndorf, snow was falling lightly. We found a parking place on the cobblestone streets close to the small white church. Villagers were arriving in horse-drawn carts, sleigh bells ringing merrily. Other villagers arrived on foot, strolling arm in arm. People started to enter the church. So did we.

But as we went up the steps, the greeters at the door sadly shook their heads. The church was only large enough to hold members of the congregation and the villagers of Oberndorf.

We had traveled all this way to celebrate Christmas in this church, and now we could not even go inside.

The light snow ceased its gentle cascade. It began to grow colder. Steve and Don and I stood in the churchyard as the first strains of music drifted through the doors. Jason began to cry, and I snuggled the baby deeper into the folds of my coat. Now I was crying too. The homesickness, the depression that I'd begun to lose, came back.

There was a scrunch of snow. A silver-haired man approached us, gesturing toward the church door. "Come in, come in," he said. In broken English, he explained that he was one of the elders and we were invited to come in as his guests.

We stepped into the church, filled to overflowing, glowing with candlelight and alive with the sound of caroling. But then, as the music swelled, Jason began to cry. I tried to hush him. He cried even harder. I was embarrassed. Would we continue to be welcome now?

I felt a hand on my arm and turned. A tiny, wizened old woman behind us was reaching out for the baby. I shook my head no, but she leaned over and gently took Jason from me. I watched anxiously as she rocked him in her arms and smiled. Jason stopped crying and smiled back at her. He seemed contented, so I stopped worrying.

As yet another carol began, I turned and looked again. But Jason was no longer in the old woman's arms!

I gasped. But the woman nodded and gestured across the row. My eyes rapidly scanned the pews. Jason was now several rows away, being passed slowly from one person to the next. As the contented bundle was moved along, I heard whispers explaining, "*Americanisches Kind, americanisches Kind...*"

"Relax," Steve whispered. "Enjoy the service. Jason is fine."

Silent night, holy night...

The words filled the sanctuary. With this quiet song of reverence we were welcoming the Christ Child to His world just as surely as my own baby was at this moment being welcomed to his. Jason was in the loving arms of a family, a family every bit as real as my own family in America. God's family.

... Sleep in heavenly peace...

I slipped my arms through Steve's, and he drew me close.

... Sleep in heavenly peace.

*The past is but the beginning of a beginning, and
all that is and has been is but the twilight of the dawn.*

– H.G. WELLS

DAD'S CHRISTMAS PECANS

JUDYE REILLY

I didn't know what to expect as my bus pulled into Parsons, Kansas. Why had I come 600 miles to see my father after all these years? I hadn't laid eyes on him since I was nine. Would he even recognize me at twenty? *God, let me feel some connection to him,* I prayed.

Stepping onto the platform, I spotted him standing head and shoulders above the crowd. *So he really was tall back then.* I'd wondered if his height was just the fantasy of a little girl who missed her dad. I gave him an awkward hug. "Nice to see you," he said.

We went straight to a honky-tonk three blocks from the station. "Hi, Ted!" a group of men called when we stepped into the dark bar. Clearly Dad was a regular.

He had been in and out of veterans hospitals after World War II. My mother finally divorced him, and when she remarried, he stayed away. "The war really changed him," was all the explanation one of my aunts was willing to offer. Mom refused to talk about him at all.

"Guess who this is?" Dad said to his buddies. The men looked at me and shook their heads. They had no idea. He reached into his wallet and pulled out a dog-eared baby picture of me. Holding it up to each man's nose, he asked, "Don't you recognize her? This is my princess!"

"Well, what do you know!" one of the men exclaimed. "We finally get to meet Judye." Dad had told them my name?

"She sure has grown up to be a fine young lady," another said, patting Dad on the back. "Just like you always brag, Ted." My eyes followed the ragged baby picture back into my father's wallet. I couldn't imagine what he'd said about me. We barely knew each other.

After joining the men for a drink (I had a soda), we left the bar and sat under a tree by Dad's trailer. "Do you like pecans?" he asked, shelling one from the tree. He handed me the two perfect halves of meat. Then he shelled another. He made it look so easy, peeling the nuts without crumbling the delicate meat inside. I ate as quickly as he shelled, and Dad seemed pleased. "Remember that summer you stayed at the homestead?" he asked. I'd spent the summer I was five on the farm where he grew up. "You rode those horses from sunup to sundown. You still like horses?" I said I did. Dad nodded and we got quiet again. Later he played guitar and sang as the sun set. It was as if we had no past to work out, no future to plan. He didn't try to explain, and I couldn't bring myself to ask the question that had burned inside me for years: *Why did you leave me?* My trip came to nothing, really. When I left Kansas I still felt removed from him.

That Christmas a metal tin arrived in the mail. It was full of shelled pecans. All whole, none broken. I popped one into my mouth and couldn't help but see Dad carefully preparing this package for me. I called to thank him, and he promised to keep in touch. But months went by without a word from him. *Okay,* I thought, eating the last of the pecans. *If this is all you can do, I'll try to make it enough.*

The next Christmas another tin of pecans arrived. Eventually I came to accept that the only thing about Dad I could count on was those Christmas pecans. I snacked on them while I was single, set them out for company when I was married, and baked them into cookies after I had children. Surprisingly, I came to depend on those pecans. Finally Dad was a constant, if small, presence in my life.

I was going through a difficult divorce when he died suddenly in 1985, and I didn't have many tears to spare on a father I barely knew. Slowly, I rebuilt my life and married a wonderful man, Joe. As our first Christmas together approached, I decided to bake some holiday treats. I opened the kitchen cabinet and reached for the tin of pecans. *How silly of me,* I thought. Dad had been dead for three years. There were no pecans in my pantry.

Staring at the shelf, I felt empty. I'd never told Joe about Dad's pecans. How could I explain what they'd meant to me? I started to cry. For the first time ever, I cried because my father wasn't in my life.

By the time my children came home from school, I had pulled myself together. "Who wants to help me make cookies?" I asked. *They won't be quite the same*, I thought. *Not without pecans.* Suddenly the back door opened and Joe bounded in with a big grin. "I have something for you," he said, holding his hands behind his back.

"What is it?" I asked. With a flourish, Joe dropped to one knee and presented me with a plastic bag full of nuts. I turned the bag over in my hands. Shelled pecans, all in neat halves, no broken pieces. I started crying all over again. Joe wrapped his arms around me. "What's wrong?" he asked. "I thought you liked pecans. A guy was selling them at work."

I smiled at Joe. "It's a long story," I said. And I told him all of it.

*More than the gift, you must see the love with which
it is given.*
—AUTHOR UNKNOWN

EVERYBODY'S CHILD

ELEANOR SASS

I was an only child. In addition to my parents and three grandparents, I had eight aunts and eight uncles all living within a short distance of one another. Some were married, but none had any children, so I became everybody's child. This was usually a wonderful thing—especially around Christmas and my birthday—but it could also be an ordeal, with twenty-one adults focusing on me and not always agreeing on what was best.

For instance, the time Mama signed me up for piano lessons, Aunt Helen, who adored the ballet, insisted dance lessons were better. "It will give her grace," she declared. Mama tried to explain why piano was her preference. Helen wouldn't relent. It was like watching a game of tennis. Eventually I played piano and danced.

Then there were the differences between my father and his brother Lou. Uncle Lou, a lifelong bachelor, lived with my grandparents in a house just across the street from ours in Queens, New York. He introduced me to two of his passions—gardening and golf. He also gave me a green bicycle—my first two-wheeler. Lou thought I was old enough at age eight to ride in the street. Daddy disagreed. "There's too much traffic," he argued.

"I know Eleanor," Uncle Lou retorted. "She'll be careful!"

Aunt Billie, who was often the family mediator, finally intervened. She suggested Daddy and I go with the shiny new bike to a nearby park, where Daddy could evaluate my skill.

"On the way back," she suggested, "let Eleanor ride in light traffic and see for yourself if she's up to it." After several trips to the park, Daddy decided he could trust me to ride by myself in the street.

Once, when I was a young teen, several other members of my church youth group and I were caught trying cigarettes. I had to endure more than a dozen separate lectures on the evils of tobacco. But it cured my curiosity about smoking.

One of the most powerful memories I have from my childhood is the Christmas when I was four. Weeks before, my family had decided I should have the gift every little girl dreams of—a dollhouse. But this would be no run-of-the-mill dollhouse.

Daddy and Uncle Charlie paid a visit to the local lumberyard. They bought some plywood, then drove across the George Washington Bridge to Uncle Ben's place in Palisades Park, New York. Uncle Ben, who had a fully-equipped woodworking shop, cut out the frame on a special jigsaw.

Back in Queens they set up the frame in the basement of Uncle Paul's house—which happened to be right next door to ours. I recall wondering why Uncle Paul had hung shades on his basement windows, but I didn't question him about it. Like most kids my age, I thought Santa brought all those lovely gifts on Christmas morning. The back and front of the dollhouse were removable. An ornate staircase ran from the first floor to the third floor. The outside was painted a bright yellow and crowned with a dark-green roof.

As the men hammered and painted, the women in the family sewed and trimmed. Every window of the dollhouse was curtained, every room wall-papered. Aunt Billie, who lived with Uncle Charlie in the house on the other side of mine, was an interior decorator. She took charge of the color coordination and carpeting. Aunt Emma created the most beautiful yellow chiffon and silk bassinet for the nursery. The guest bedroom was done in blue and white. If you looked closely you could see that the small end tables on either side of the double bed were empty thread spools painted blue and white. The bed itself was a block of wood covered with blue satin and white lace.

My mother and her mother (Grandma Parry, who lived in Oradell, New Jersey) worked on the living room. The finishing touches were a china spaniel lying on the carpet near the fireplace and a tiny glass Christmas tree atop the polished baby grand piano.

A gentle snowfall ushered in Christmas Eve. Mama got me to bed early. After saying my prayers in record time (I couldn't wait for morning to come), I closed my eyes tight and somehow willed myself to sleep. Only a few hours later, though, I was awakened by a noisy chorus of "Good-bye, Santa! Thanks, Santa! See you next year, Santa!" *What's going on?* I wondered. It's not even light out yet. Then the lamp on my dresser flicked on and Mama was beside me, urging me into my robe and slippers so I could "come see what Santa brought."

In our living room I was overwhelmed by what seemed to be wall-to-wall adults. Still hazy with sleep, I thought, *Who are these people?* As I rubbed my eyes, the faces began to register—Grandma and Grandpa Sass, Grandma Parry, every one of my aunts and uncles. *What are they all doing here?* We were a close family, but it was only a very special event that brought us all together. Then I saw Daddy sitting on the floor next to the Christmas tree. He motioned for me to come over and began to unhook the back of what looked like. . . a dollhouse!

I remember it almost as a dream, a warm, wonderful dream that even after more than half a century is as vivid as if I just awakened from it. It was several years before I understood that Santa didn't really bring the dollhouse. And, really, the dollhouse wasn't the true gift that Christmas. I understood that in my heart as I gazed around at all my relatives that long-ago night. God had truly given me the greatest gift of all—a strong, loving family, each and every one of them an angel watching over me.

Songs have power to quiet the restless pulse of care,
and come like a benediction that follows after prayer.
—HENRY WADSWORTH LONGFELLOW

HEAVENLY MUSIC

RICHARD W. O'DONNELL

On a bright spring morning in 1854, Ludwig Eck sat down to breakfast in a quaint Prussian inn near the Austrian border. As master of the Royal Court Choir in Berlin, Eck had been given a special task: Track down the composer of the favorite hymn of the King of Prussia, Friedrich Wilhelm IV. Though "The Song From Heaven" was known all over the continent, it had no attribution in the songbooks. "I must know the composer's name!" declared the king.

Eck traveled across Prussia and neighboring countries on horseback. He investigated every rumor, and even rumors of rumors, that came his way about "The Song From Heaven." The search had exhausted him, and he had neglected his work as concertmaster. After seven years, he was still no closer to finding out who wrote the heavenly music so beloved by the king. He was just returning from yet another failed attempt. Eck tried to concentrate on the meal before him, but the thought of again disappointing His Majesty ruined his appetite.

Reaching for his coffee, Eck heard an all-too-familiar melody being whistled in the air above him. The king's hymn? He wondered if, after all this time, he had begun humming the tune without even knowing it. Nevertheless, he twisted around in his chair and slowly raised his eyes toward the ceiling. The sound did seem to be coming from above his head.

There Eck noticed for the first time a wrought-iron cage holding a little black-and-white bird—a bullfinch, if he wasn't mistaken. The bird was sitting on its perch, happily singing. Eck cocked his ear toward the cage. Could it be true? This delightful creature was serenading him with the very song he had been searching for.

Across the room, the waiter noticed the expression on Eck's face. He hurried to the table. "Shall I remove the bird, sir?" the waiter asked.

"That song!" Eck nearly shouted. "The bird is singing the king's favorite hymn. Could you tell me where that bird came from?"

"I will check with the innkeeper," the waiter offered, and rushed off to find the owner.

Eck pushed away the buttered rolls and marmalade. He was too excited to eat. He drummed his fingers on the table, the bird warbling all the while. Finally the waiter returned.

"Yes?" Eck asked eagerly.

"The bullfinch was purchased from young Felix Gruber, a student at St. Peter's Abbey across the Austrian border." Eck shook the waiter's hand and got up from the table. No time for breakfast now. Within the hour, Eck's horse was ready, and he was on his way to the abbey in Salzburg. The abbot at St. Peter's was not pleased to hear about the bird. "I am not in favor of caging one of God's creatures," he said.

"If you'll pardon me, I must speak to Felix Gruber," requested the concertmaster. "I am here on His Majesty's business." The abbot sniffed, then nodded to his assistant.

Minutes later the fifteen-year-old boy was brought before Eck. "Yes, sir," the boy said, eyeing the abbot nervously, "I caught the bullfinch and taught it to sing the song."

"Who taught you the song, young man?"

"My father," said the youth. Eck grew impatient. The father had, no doubt, learned it from someone else, and so on down the line. Eck would visit each person named, and in the end wind up where he had started with no idea who had created the melody. "And where did your father learn the song?" Eck asked halfheartedly.

"My father," said Felix Gruber with a trace of pride, "didn't have to learn the song. He wrote the music. His friend, Father Josef Mohr, wrote the words."

The concertmaster almost leaped with joy, but he was far too dignified. "I would be honored to meet Herr Gruber," Eck said. "I have waited a long time."

One week later, Eck arrived in the Austrian village of Hallein, where the elder Gruber was the organist at the local church. "Yes, I wrote the music," Franz Gruber said, surprised to be receiving a visit from the Royal Concertmaster himself. Eck pressed him: When? Where? Under what circumstances? For a specific occasion? Eck wanted all the details for the king.

Gruber obliged. "In 1818, I was the organist at St. Nicholas's Church in Oberndorf," he began. "When the organ broke down on Christmas Eve, it seemed we would not have any music at our Christmas service. Father Mohr had written a poem about the birth of Christ. At his request, I immediately put music to the words. I had never worked so fast in all my life. But I was pleased with the result and performed it on guitar at midnight Mass."

The organ at St. Nicholas continued to break down. Since it could only be properly fixed by the itinerant repairman who came once every spring, it seemed the old instrument was broken more often than not. Finally, years after Gruber's midnight guitar performance on Christmas Eve, the church commissioned a man named Carl Mauracher to build a brand-new organ. While he was working in the choir loft, he came across a handwritten copy of Gruber's song and took the sheet music back to his home in the Ziller Valley. Soon people were singing the song at Christmastime throughout the Tyrolean Mountains. From there, the song spread.

"The song is known all over Europe," Eck informed the composer.

"Is it?" Gruber said, surprised.

Eck smiled at the organist. "That is why I have searched seven years for you, sir," he said. "The King of Prussia has been waiting a long time to know the composer of 'The Song From Heaven.'"

Gruber was puzzled. "The Song From Heaven?"

"That is what people call your song in Europe," the concertmaster explained. "What do you call it?"

"We call it by the title of Father Mohr's poem," said Gruber. "We call it 'Silent Night.'"

Eck was anxious to report to the king, but on the way back to Berlin he made a quick stop. "A successful journey?" the waiter asked when Eck entered the dining room at the inn near the border.

"Yes, thank you," Eck replied. "But I have one more request." He pricked his ears for the bird's song. "I would like to buy the bullfinch."

The innkeeper agreed, and Eck asked if the songbird had been named. It had not. "I'll take care of that!" Eck said, carrying the bird home with him to Berlin.

With his quest finally over, Eck resumed his duties with the Royal Choir and devoted himself to making music once more. King Friedrich Wilhelm IV never forgot the good work his concertmaster had done. Year-round the bullfinch serenaded Eck with "Silent Night." During the part where "heavenly hosts sing hallelujah," Eck imagined his songbird among them. For he had named his winged messenger Angel. It was she who had heralded the end of his journey.

The Son of man shall send forth his angels...
—MATTHEW 13:41

LONG WALK HOME

MARGARET NEWTON

T he traps are set," my husband, Claude, announced.

Seven-year-old Don tugged his winter boots off and headed to the window, watching for the snow he hoped would fall this Christmas Eve. "Maybe we'll catch some beavers," he said.

Claude nodded and took off his coat. He had never set traps before. In fact, he had never gone hunting or fishing. Usually Claude and Don spent time together reading or bowling, but Claude had started to think he should do something more "macho" with our growing son. Most of Don's friends hunted with their fathers and sold the pelts at the local trading post. In 1955 that was a popular way to pick up extra money in rural Oregon. Claude didn't want Don to feel like he was missing out, so he borrowed some traps from a neighbor and took Don across the pasture to the irrigation ditch to set them. Now it looked like Claude was having second thoughts.

Just past sunset Don let out an excited shout. "It's snowing!" he cried. "The biggest flakes you've ever seen!" I grabbed my camera, and the three of us went outside. After we came back in, Claude stood staring out the window.

I went to start dinner, and Don followed me into the kitchen to set the table. Moments later Claude appeared in the doorway. "Let's go down and spring those traps," he said. I was glad. Dinner could wait.

"Okay," Don agreed cheerfully, pulling on his boots. I got my coat. We sang carols to pass the time while walking back across the pasture. Don admitted he didn't care if he ever caught a beaver—or any other animal, for that matter. Claude said that was just fine. I prayed it wasn't too late. Finally the three of us stood hand in hand beside the ditch.

"All empty," Claude said, relief in his voice. He sprang each trap with a stick and swung the bunch of them over his shoulder for the long walk home. The moon lit a path at our feet, and the three of us followed it through the woods in silence. Don skipped along just ahead. The trees, the moon, the snow—it was perfect, but it was more than that. There was something different about the woods that night. Something all around us, familiar and strange at the same time. It was almost as if someone else were taking our path, walking beside us. I couldn't begin to describe it, not even to Claude.

When we got home, Don sprawled out under the Christmas tree to watch the blinking lights. "How about a cup of tea?" I asked my husband, still trying to find a way to describe the presence in the woods. Claude's eyes softened, and a little smile played at the corner of his mouth. "What is it?" I asked.

"I think Jesus walked with us tonight," he said.

"Oh! Is that who it was, Daddy?" Don piped up. "I thought it was an angel."

My husband and son had found just the words I was looking for.

Faith and love will lead to miracles.
—AUTHOR UNKNOWN

THE TOUCH OF THE ANGEL'S WINGS

IDELLA BODIE

It was Christmas Eve. Elizabeth sat on the edge of her little daughter's bed. She bent over and kissed the rose-petaled cheek. With golden-flax hair spreading over the pillow and long lashes heavy with sleep, Marya looked for all the world like an angel.

Elizabeth's heart swelled with love and overflowed with the sweet joy of sharing. On this, the holiest night, she had told her little daughter about the visit of the angel.

The two of them had sat listening to the delicate Swedish chimes and watching the little angels dance round and round above the glow of magical candles. The first Christmas after Marya was born, Elizabeth's mother had given her the family keepsake. "Because you always loved it so," her mother had said.

Earlier, as Elizabeth saw the glow of the candles reflected in her little daughter's blue eyes, she felt the tender excitement mounting until the two of them and the candles were one. And Elizabeth knew it was time to share her marvelous secret.

With joy swelling even greater, Elizabeth remembered the first Christmas the angel had given her the joy of the Christmas season.

She was about Marya's age the evening she sat at the table long after the dishes had been cleared away. With her chin cupped in her hands, she followed the movement of the angels and the light tinkling of the chimes.

"Elizabeth is enchanted by those angel chimes," her mother announced to no one in particular.

It was that night Elizabeth was awakened by the soft whir-r-r.

Moonlight shimmered through the curtains of her bedroom window like the lace on her grandmother's dresses. Elizabeth lay very still. Then in the soft darkness she saw the angel—one of them from the chimes—moving around her room. Moonlight frosted the tips of the angel's wings, and the tiny horn at her mouth made the softest of sounds like twinkling bits of laughter.

Suddenly a silver magic enveloped the room, making Elizabeth's heart tremble. But she was not afraid. Under covers streaked by moonlight she marveled at the angel's fluttering. She saw the gossamer wings brush the dolls on the trunk against tile wall, her dollhouse, the edges of her storybooks, her clothes. And with the touch the whole room became a place of heavenly sweetness.

And then as quietly as the enchantment had come, it disappeared. The whirring stopped and the angel was gone. Yet a glory shone over the room until Elizabeth fell asleep again.

The next morning, it was as if the angel's wings had cleansed and blessed the world. How new everything looked! The faces of her dolls were clear and bright. Even the air smelled clean. It was as if Elizabeth was seeing and feeling everything for the first time. Her whole world was different—it had been touched by the angel's wings.

Eager to share, she had burst into the kitchen where her parents and brothers had already gathered around the breakfast table.

"Last night," she began, pointing to the little angels standing frozen in their angelic poses, "one of the angels came to my room and. . . "

"Yeah, Elizabeth." Her brothers' laughter cut across her beautiful story.

"Boys!" her mother reprimanded. "Elizabeth has a vivid imagination." And Elizabeth thought she detected a trace of a smile at the corner of her father's mouth.

Even so, the angel's touch filled the Christmas season with wonder and magic. On other Christmases the angel's coming was never quite the same. Once or twice she heard the whirring or the faint tooting of the horn. Another time she saw the moonlight frosting gossamer wings in flight. But Elizabeth knew the little angel always came and that the coming gave the world a special glow of miracles.

And tonight, after carrying this beautiful secret in her heart for all these years, she had shared it with her very own little girl. Now the beauty and magic of the angel's touch would live forever as it passed from heart to heart in love.

Those without faith might say it was just a dream, but Elizabeth knew that she had been chosen by God to be blessed with the gift of the angel's visit. For only those who believe can know the touch of the angel's wings and the miracles it brings. For in them Christ is born again each Christmas.

Perhaps tonight Marya would be awakened by the soft whir of wings.

Prayer is the voice of faith.
–RICHARD HENRY HORNE

SHE KEPT HER PROMISE

JOHN MARKAS

The experience happened when I was thirteen and seemed hardly worth telling anyone at the time. But now, ten years later, it stands above any other Christmas memory I have.

There were 118 customers on my paper route in Morganton, North Carolina. As Christmas drew near, I began to nudge my customers into a "remember the paper boy" mood. I bought 118 cheap Christmas cards, signed them "Your friendly paper boy," and several days before Christmas inserted one card in each paper.

The results were quite satisfactory—in fact, almost spectacular. The standard reply was a dollar bill slipped into an envelope marked "paper boy."

Except for Mrs. Luke Woodbury, a widow known for her devoutness. Mrs. Woodbury was standing at the door when I arrived with her Christmas paper.

"I wanted to thank you personally, Johnny, for your card," she said. "It was a kind and thoughtful act to an old lady."

The warmth of her greeting made me feel a little uneasy.

"I haven't much to give you," she said, handing me a few coins, "but I do want you to know this: I see you every day when you pass the house. Every day I will pray for you, Johnny. I will pray that God will help you and guide you wherever you go, whatever you do."

She put her hand on my shoulder, almost like a caress, and then went back into her house.

A thirteen-year-old is more inclined to be uncomfortable than moved by such an experience. I certainly didn't think too much about it at the time. Nor did I have any undue interest in religion.

In the years that followed, I saw Mrs. Woodbury on a few occasions. She always smiled at me in a meaningful way. When I went to Duke University, I forgot about Mrs. Woodbury until…

Until two years ago when the turning point in my life came at a Fellowship of Christian Athletes' conference. A perfunctory Christian until then, I stepped from the darkness of ordinary living into the brightness and joyousness of a new life with Christ at the center.

Soon after this experience, I was giving a talk in Chattanooga in which I re-evaluated my life. I spoke about how lucky I was. For the truth of the matter is that I have had to work very hard for my "C" average in college. As for football, during my high school and early college years I had been short of both weight and talent. Yet somehow I was able to find within myself the extra strength or ability I needed to do what had to be done.

After church a lady told me:

"That was not luck; you've obviously had some people praying hard for you all this time."

This was a sudden new thought. My parents, of course. Their faith had always been strong.

And then I remembered Mrs. Woodbury—and her promise to pray for me. How much I owed her!

A few months ago I discovered that Mrs. Woodbury had entered a home where she could get special care. As a tribute to her—and all the unselfish, thoughtful people who pray for others—I tell this story of what I now consider my most memorable Christmas.

A perfect cause must produce a perfect effect.
−ERNEST HOLMES

A STRING OF BLUE BEADS

FULTON OURSLER

Pete Richards was the loneliest man in town on the day Jean Grace opened the door to his shop. Pete's small business had come down to him from his grandfather. The little front window was strewn with a disarray of old-fashioned things: bracelets and lockets worn in days before the Civil War, gold rings and silver boxes, images of jade and ivory, porcelain figurines.

On this winter's afternoon a child was standing there, her forehead against the glass, earnest and enormous eyes studying each discarded treasure as if she were looking for something quite special. Finally she straightened up with a satisfied air and entered the store.

The shadowy interior of Pete Richards' establishment was even more cluttered than his show window. Shelves were stacked with jewel caskets, dueling pistols, clocks and lamps, and the floor was heaped with andirons and mandolins and things hard to find a name for.

Behind the counter stood Pete himself, a man not more than thirty, but with hair already turning gray. There was a bleak air about him as he looked at the small customer who flattened her ungloved hands on the counter.

"Mister," she began, "would you please let me look at that string of blue beads in the window?"

Pete parted the draperies and lifted out a necklace. The turquoise stones gleamed brightly against the pallor of his palm as he spread the ornament before her.

"They're just perfect," said the child, entirely to herself. "Will you wrap them up pretty for me, please?"

Pete studied her with a stony air. "Are you buying these for someone?"

"They're for my big sister. She takes care of me. You see, this will be the first Christmas since Mother died. I've been looking for the most wonderful Christmas present for my sister."

"How much money do you have?" asked Pete warily.

She had been busily untying the knots in a handkerchief, and now she poured out a handful of pennies on the counter.

"I emptied my bank," she explained simply.

Pete Richards looked at her thoughtfully. Then he carefully drew back the necklace; the price tag was visible to him but not to her. How could he tell her? The trusting look of her blue eyes smote him like the pain of an old wound.

"Just a minute," he said, and turned toward the back of the store. Over his shoulder he called, "What's your name?" He was very busy about something.

"Jean Grace."

When Pete returned to where Jean Grace waited, a package lay in his hand, wrapped in scarlet paper and tied with a bow of green ribbon. "There you are," he said shortly. "Don't lose it on the way home."

She smiled happily at him over her shoulder as she ran out the door. Through the window he watched her go, while desolation flooded his thoughts. Something about Jean Grace and her string of beads had stirred him to the depths of a grief that would not stay buried. The child's hair was wheat yellow, her eyes sea blue, and once upon a time, not long before, Pete had been in love with a girl with hair of that same yellow and with eyes just as blue. And the turquoise necklace was to have been hers.

But there had come a rainy night—a truck skidding on a slippery road—and the life was crushed out of his dream.

Since then, Pete Richards had lived too much with his grief in solitude. He was politely attentive to customers, but after business hours his world seemed irrevocably empty.

The blue eyes of Jean Grace jolted him into acute remembrance of what he had lost. The pain of it made him recoil from the exuberance of holiday shoppers. During the next ten days trade was brisk; chattering women swarmed in, fingering trinkets, trying to bargain. When the last customer had gone, late on Christmas Eve, he sighed with relief. It was over for another year. But for Pete Richards the night was not quite over.

The door opened and a young woman hurried in. With an inexplicable start, he realized that she looked familiar, yet he could not remember when or where he had seen her before. Her hair was golden yellow and her large eyes were blue. Without speaking, she drew from her purse a package loosely unwrapped in its red paper, a bow of green ribbon with it. Presently the string of blue beads lay gleaming again before him.

"Did this come from your shop?" she asked.

Pete raised his eyes to hers and answered softly, "Yes, it did."

"Are the stones real?"

"Yes. Not the finest quality—but real."

"Can you remember who it was you sold them to?"

"She was a small girl. Her name was Jean. She bought them for her older sister's Christmas present."

"How much are they worth?"

"The price," he told her solemnly, "is always a confidential matter between the seller and the customer."

"But Jean has never had more than a few pennies of spending money. How could she pay for them?"

Pete was folding the gay paper back into its creases, rewrapping the little package just as neatly as before.

"She paid the biggest price anyone can ever pay," he said. "She gave all she had."

There was a silence then that filled the little curio shop. In some faraway steeple, a bell began to ring. The sound of the distant chiming, the little package lying on the counter, the question in the eyes of the girl, and the strange feeling of renewal struggling unreasonably in the heart of the man all had come to be because of the love of a child.

"But why did you do it?"

He held out the gift in his hand.

"It's already Christmas morning," he said "and it's my misfortune that I have no one to give anything to. Will you let me see you home and wish you a Merry Christmas at your door?"

And so, to the sound of many bells, and in the midst of happy people, Pete Richards and a girl whose name he had yet to learn walked out into the beginning of the great day that brings hope into the world for us all.

All God's angels come to us disguised.

–JAMES RUSSELL LOWELL

THE STRANGER AT TABLE NO. 5

CORYNE WONG-COLLINSWORTH

It was five days before Christmas, and the cafe where I worked in northern California glowed with strands of red and green chili peppers. Holiday music played over the sound system, and my co-workers excitedly discussed their plans. "Doing anything special?" they asked me. I shook my head no.

I was 3,000 miles from my family in Hawaii, pursuing my lifelong dream of becoming a pediatric nurse. I attended classes all day, then went straight to my full-time waitress job at night. My weekly schedule left me exhausted and extremely homesick.

I had always looked forward to the holidays. But this December I felt unable to go on. In my prayers I told God that if I could just get home to see my mom, dad, and brothers, I could survive the next two years until I graduated. But how? Rent, tuition, textbooks, and other expenses left me with no extra cash. Money to go home? I barely had money to eat.

"I'm on my break. Cover for me, will you?" asked Maribelle, another waitress, as she passed me on her way to the employees' lounge. "By the way, there's this guy at table five," she said. "He's been sitting there for more than an hour, not making any trouble but not ordering anything either." She paused. "It's like he's. . . waiting for somebody."

I looked in the corner. Sure enough, there was a slim, pleasant-looking man dressed in worn Levis, a red-and-black plaid shirt, and a black baseball cap, just sitting, alone. I went over, trying to muster a smile. "I'm Cory," I said. "Please let me know if you want anything."

I was turning to walk away when the man spoke. He had a soft, low voice, but somehow I could hear it clear and plain in the noisy restaurant. "I'd like an order of nachos," he said. "And a glass of water."

My heart sank. The nachos were the cheapest thing on the menu, which meant I wouldn't get much of a tip. But maybe this guy was broke, and I sure knew how that felt. So I tried my best to make him feel okay. "Coming right up," I said. I returned a few minutes later and slid the nachos in front of him. "That will be two dollars and ninety-five cents."

He reached into his pocket and handed me a single bill. "Keep the change," he said quietly.

I looked—then looked again. "Excuse me, sir," I said. "This is a hundred-dollar bill."

"I know," he replied gently.

My eyes opened wide. "I don't understand," I said. "What do you want from me?"

"Not a thing," he said, looking straight into my eyes. He stood up. "Call your mother tonight," he said. "Merry Christmas." Then he moved off in the direction of the front door. When I turned to thank him, he was nowhere in sight, although the exit was at least fifty feet away.

The rest of the evening passed in a blur. I finished work, went back to my apartment, and put the money on the table. I had just turned on the television when the phone rang. It was my mother! She announced that my brothers had bought an airline ticket to get me home for Christmas. But they could only afford the fare one way. "Can you possibly manage the other part of the ticket?" she asked.

At that moment a commercial flashed on television. A major airline was announcing cut-rate fares to Hawaii, one way for ninety-nine dollars! I jumped off the sofa, shouting, "Thank you, God. I'm going home!"

That was seven years ago. Because of that visit to my family, I returned to my studies filled with new spirit and determination. Today I'm a registered nurse, caring for sick children. And every Christmas, my husband, John, and I try to do something for someone else, just as the man at table number five had done for me. One year we purchased packages of warm socks and, with the wind howling at our backs, crept along the creek and handed them out to the people without homes who resided on the banks. The following Christmas we organized a blanket drive; and as the homeless gathered around a campfire, wrapped in their new blankets, John asked each to reflect on the tiny babe whose birthday it was.

Whether creeping along creek beds, tiptoeing down hospital corridors to hang stockings, or secretly leaving gifts of food (who knows where this Christmas will find us?), I always think of the mysterious stranger who helped me.

In my time of need he appeared—no halo or sparkling wings, but a sort of angel just the same. And that is the kind of angel we all can be.

*If someone listens, or stretches out a hand, or whispers
a kind word of encouragement, or attempts to understand
a lonely person, extraordinary things begin to happen.*
—LORETTA GIORZARTIS

A SONG FOR ELIZABETH

ROBIN COLE

ecember snow swept across the parking lot of Crescent Manor Convalescent Home. As the youngest nurse on the staff, I sat with the charge nurse at the North Wing station, staring out the double-glass doors and waiting for the first wave of evening visitors. At the sound of bedroom slippers flapping against bare heels, I turned to see Elizabeth, one of our patients, striding down the corridor.

"Oh, please," groaned the charge nurse, "not tonight! Not when we're shorthanded already!"

Rounding the corner, Elizabeth jerked the sash of her tired chenille robe tighter around her skinny waist. We hadn't combed her hair for a while, and it made a scraggly halo around her wrinkled face.

"Doop doop," she said, nodding quickly and hurrying on. "Doop doop," she said to the man in the dayroom slumped in front of the TV, a belt holding him in his wheelchair.

The charge nurse turned to me. "Can you settle her down?"

"Shall I go after her or wait till she comes around again?"

"Just wait. I may need you here before she gets back. She never does any harm. It's just that ridiculous sound she makes. I wonder if she thinks she's saying words!"

A group of visitors swept through the front doors. They came in, scraping feet on the rug, shaking snow from their coats, cleaning their glasses. They clustered around the desk, seeking information, and as they did Elizabeth came striding by again. "Doop doop," she said happily to everyone. I moved out to intercept the purposeful strider.

"Elizabeth," I said, taking her bony elbow, "I need you to do something for me. Come and sit down and I'll tell you about it." I was stalling. This wasn't anything I had learned in training, but I would think of *something*.

The charge nurse stared at me and, shaking her head, turned her attention to the group of visitors surrounding the desk. Nobody ever got Elizabeth to do anything. We counted it a good day if we could keep her from pacing the halls.

Elizabeth stopped. She looked into my face with a puzzled frown. "Doop doop," she said.

I led her to a writing table in the dayroom and found a piece of paper and a pencil.

"Sit down here at the desk, Elizabeth. Write your name for me."

Her watery eyes grew cloudy. Deep furrows appeared between her brows. She took the stubby pencil in her gnarled hand and held it above the paper. Again and again she looked at the paper and then at me questioningly.

"Here. I'll write it first, and then you can copy it, okay?"

In large, clear script, I wrote, "Elizabeth Goode."

"There you are. You stay here and copy that. I'll be right back."

At the edge of the dayroom I turned, half expecting to see her following me, but she sat quietly, pencil in hand. The only sound now came from the muffled voices of visitors and their ailing loved ones.

"Elizabeth is writing," I told the charge nurse. I could hardly believe it.

"Fantastic," she said calmly. "You'd better not leave her alone for long. We don't have time to clean pencil marks off the walls tonight." She turned away, avoiding my eyes. "Oh, I almost forgot—Novak and Sellers both have the flu. They'll be out all week. Looks like you'll be working Christmas Eve." She pulled a metal-backed chart from the file and was suddenly very busy.

I swallowed hard. Until now I had loved my independence, my own small trailer. At twenty-two I was just out of nurse's training and on my own. But I had never spent Christmas Eve away from my parents and my brothers. That wasn't in the picture at all when I moved away from home. I planned to go home for holidays.

Words raced through my head: *They'll go to the candlelight service without me! They'll read the stories, and I won't be there to hear! What kind of Christmas can I have in a little trailer with nothing to decorate but a potted fern? How can it be Christmas if I can't be the first one up to turn on the tree lights? Who'll make the cocoa for the family?*

Tears burned my eyes, but I blinked them back. Nodding slowly, I walked toward the dayroom.

Elizabeth sat at the writing table staring down at the paper in front of her. Softly I touched my hand to her fragile shoulder, and she looked up with a smile. She handed me the paper. Under my big, bold writing was a wobbly signature.

"Elizabeth Goode," it read.

"Doop doop," said Elizabeth with satisfaction.

Later that night, when all the visitors were gone and the North Wing was dark and silent, I sat with the charge nurse, completing charts. "Do you suppose I could take Elizabeth out tomorrow?" I asked. In good weather, we often took the patients for walks or rides, but I didn't know about snowy nights. "I'd like to go to Christmas Eve service, and I think she'd like to go with me."

"Wouldn't she be a problem? What about the doop doop?"

"I think I can explain it to her. You know, nobody else talks during church, so she'd probably be quiet too. Look how well she did this afternoon when I gave her something to do."

The charge nurse looked thoughtful. "Things would be a lot easier around here if you did take her. Then you could get her ready for bed when you got back. There'll be visitors to help with the others, but nobody has been here for Elizabeth in a long time. I'll ask her doctor for you."

And so it was that a first-year nurse and a tall, skinny old lady arrived at First Church on Christmas Eve just before the service began. The snow had stopped and the stars were brilliant in the clear, cold sky.

"Now, Elizabeth," I said, "I don't know how much you can understand, but listen to me. We're going in to sit down with the rest of the people. There'll be music and someone will read. There'll be kids in costumes too. But we aren't going to say anything. We'll stand up when it's time to sing, and we'll hold the hymnal together."

Elizabeth looked grave. "Doop doop," she said.

Oh, Lord, I hope she understands! I thought. Suppose she gets up and heads down the aisle wishing everyone a doop doop?

I wrapped Elizabeth's coat and shawl around her and tucked my arm under hers. Together we entered the candlelit church. Elizabeth's watery old eyes gleamed, and her face crinkled in a smile. But she said nothing.

The choir entered singing. The pastor read the Christmas story from the Bible: "And there were, in the same country, shepherds. . . "

Costumed children took their places at the front of the church dressed as shepherds and wise men, angels and the holy family. Elizabeth watched, but she said nothing. The congregation rose to sing "Joy to the World." Elizabeth stood, holding the hymnal with me, her mouth closed. The lights in the sanctuary dimmed, and two white-robed angels lit the candelabra. Finally the organ began the introduction to "Silent Night," and we stood again.

I handed the hymnal to Elizabeth, but she shook her head. A cold dread gathered at the back of my neck. Now what? Would this be the moment when she started wandering down the aisle? I looked at her wrinkled face out of the corner of my eye, trying to guess her thoughts. The singing began. I sang as loudly as I could, hoping to attract Elizabeth's attention. As I paused for breath, I heard a thin, cracked voice.

"Sleep in heavenly peace," it sang. "Sleep in heavenly peace."

Elizabeth! Staring straight ahead, candlelight reflected in her eyes, she was singing the words without consulting the hymnal.

> *Oh, Lord, forgive me,* I prayed. *Sometimes I forget. Of course it can be Christmas with only a fern to decorate. Of course it can be Christmas without a tree or the family or cocoa. Christmas is the story of love. It's the birth of the Son of God, and it can live in the heart and memory of a gray-haired old woman.*

"Christ the Savior is born," sang Elizabeth. "Christ the Savior is born."

"Merry Christmas, Elizabeth," I whispered, gently patting her arm.

"Doop doop," Elizabeth replied contentedly.

*Blessed be childhood, which brings down something
of heaven into the midst of our rough earthliness.*
–HENRI FRÉDÉRIC AMIEL

GOLD, CIRCUMSTANCE, AND MUD

REX KNOWLES

t was the week before Christmas. I was baby-sitting with our four older children while my wife took the baby for his checkup. Baby-sitting to me means reading the paper while the kids mess up the house.

Only that day I wasn't reading. I was fuming. As I flicked angrily through every page of the paper, gifts glittered and reindeer pranced, and I was told that there were only six more days in which to rush out and buy what I couldn't afford and nobody needed. What, I asked myself indignantly, did the glitter and the rush have to do with the birth of Christ?

There was a knock on the door of the study where I had barricaded myself. Then Nancy's voice, "Daddy, we have a play to put on. Do you want to see it?"

I didn't. But I had fatherly responsibilities, so I followed her into the living room. Right away I knew it was a Christmas play, for at the foot of the piano stool was a lighted flashlight wrapped in swaddling clothes lying in a shoe box.

Rex (age six) came in wearing my bathrobe and carrying a mop handle. He sat on the stool and looked at the flashlight. Nancy (ten) draped a sheet over her head, stood behind Rex, and began, "I'm Mary and this boy is

Joseph. Usually in this play Joseph stands up and Mary sits down. But Mary sitting down is taller than Joseph standing up, so we thought it looked better this way."

Enter Trudy (four) at a full run. She never has learned to walk. There were pillowcases over her arms. She spread them wide and said only, "I'm an angel."

Then came Anne (eight). I knew right away she represented a wise man. In the first place she moved like she was riding a camel (she had on her mother's high heels). And she was bedecked with all the jewelry available. On a pillow she carried three items, undoubtedly gold, frankincense, and myrrh.

She undulated across the room, bowed to the flashlight, to Mary, to Joseph, to the angel, and to me and then announced, "I am all three wise men. I bring precious gifts: gold, circumstance, and mud."

That was all. The play was over. I didn't laugh. I prayed. How near the truth Anne was! We come at Christmas burdened down with gold—with the showy gift and the tinselly tree. Under the circumstances we can do no other, circumstances of our time and place and custom. And it seems a bit like mud when we think of it.

But I looked at the shining faces of my children, as their audience of one applauded them, and remembered that a Child showed us how these things can be transformed. I remembered that this Child came into a material world and in so doing eternally blessed the material. He accepted the circumstances, imperfect and frustrating, into which He was born, and thereby infused them with the divine. And as for mud, to you and me it may be something to sweep off the rug, but to all children it is something to build with.

Children see so surely through the tinsel and the habit and the earthly, to the love which, in them all, strains for expression.

AUTHOR INDEX

TITLE INDEX